John

Link·Ability

4 powerful strategies to maximise your LinkedIn™ success

Thank you for everything you do and for being so relentlessly helpful.

Lynnaire

LYNNAIRE JOHNSTON

Disclaimer

The material in this publication is of the nature of general comment only, and does not represent professional advice. It is not intended to provide specific guidance for particular circumstances and it should not be relied on as the basis for any decision to take action or not take action on any matter which it covers. Readers should obtain professional advice where appropriate, before making any such decision. To the maximum extent permitted by law, the author and publisher disclaim all responsibility and liability to any person, arising directly or indirectly from any person taking or not taking action based on the information in this publication.

Contents

Introduction

Whatever your goal or ambition, this book will show you how to use LinkedIn to:

- Become the company of choice in your industry.

- Be invited to speak at international events.

- Achieve recognition as a leader in your field of expertise.

- Network with industry luminaries.

- Land the job of your dreams.

The strategies I share will enhance your business, your career and your brand. Harnessing the power of the platform will have a profound impact on your business life. Whether you are a CEO, business owner, marketing executive or any type of business professional, LinkedIn can help you achieve the success you are looking for.

It isn't difficult either. Certainly, there are some techniques to learn but once these are mastered and the four strategies I detail in this book understood and implemented, the world will be your oyster. You will be astonished at the opportunities that come your way.

There is a caveat, however. And it is this: **these strategies are based on the mindset of giving**. In order to attract success, you must be willing to help others. Whether that is through sharing your knowledge, initiating conversations and stimulating debate or facilitating introductions between interested parties, giving comes first.

With that in mind, in Link·Ability I lay out four strategies that used either separately or together, will make an enormous difference to your professional life.

These strategies are **Connecting**, **Publishing**, **Engaging** and **Direct Messaging**. There is a chapter on each in which I will show you how they work; what you can do with them; the mistakes to avoid and other techniques you rarely hear about.

What you can achieve with LinkedIn

Success means different things to each of us. It could be increased revenue, profitability or a higher salary. It could be gaining a reputation as an expert or thought leader. These are all credible and reasonable reasons for using LinkedIn. But where the platform truly excels is in shining a light on those willing to share what they know. It allows us to publish ideas, tips, recommendations, research or whatever valuable information we have that will help others. This results in kudos and cachet for the person sharing which in turn translates into credibility, visibility and most of all trust.

In his book *Give and Take: The Surprising Power of the Good Guy in a Tough World*, Adam Grant cites research showing givers outperform takers in business. That's how LinkedIn works, too. People share useful, important information that cannot be found elsewhere, without immediate or overt expectation of reward. But reward there is. And it comes in different forms.

Here are a few opportunities that have come about from my own activity on LinkedIn:

- Being invited as a guest on an international podcast.

- Forming a valuable friendship with a LinkedIn trainer in the US who is a source of inspiration.

- Setting up a small group of like-minded business professionals who help each other on LinkedIn and have, as a result, formed a tight, personal bond.

- Coaching help that has assisted my business.

- The organising and hosting of LinkedIn Local events.

- A constant stream of people wanting to do business with me in one form or another.

- The satisfaction of helping people who approach me with questions about the platform.

- The opportunity to write this book and receive help from the right people to do it.

- Working with fascinating, inspirational clients.

The opportunities that come as a result of **your** LinkedIn presence and work will be different from these. They might include meeting a long-time hero or someone you admire, being invited to write for an industry blog or publication, becoming an influencer others seek out or finding the ideal customer.

The reasons for being active on LinkedIn are endless but English scholar Dr Joy Madden breaks them into these categories:

- Promoting yourself and your activities.

- Connecting with others.

- Acquiring or accessing information.

- Business opportunities.

- Personal development and intellectual stimulation.

- Keeping in the know.

- Financial.

Dr Madden's complete list of reasons to be on LinkedIn can be found in the Appendix.

Where LinkedIn sits in the social media mix

The business world's perception of LinkedIn is changing. In the same way businesses began to realise some decades ago that having a website was a necessity, organisations and business professionals now see LinkedIn as essential. People who previously threw together a CV-style LinkedIn profile and then ignored it, now understand that LinkedIn is *the* social media platform of choice for business. And that a substandard profile does not make them look professional, capable or someone a potential employer or client might want to work with. These people may have fewer than 500 connections (widely considered to be a viable minimum), incomplete profiles and make no attempt to build authority in their area of expertise. Which is a great loss of opportunity because, when used well, LinkedIn helps build credibility and reputation, widens spheres of influence, brings in business and opens doors to myriad opportunities.

Approximate LinkedIn member numbers (as of August 2020)

- 700 million members worldwide
- 11 million in Australia
- 2 million in New Zealand
- 28 million in the UK
- 190 million in the USA
- 66 million in India

(Source: LinkedIn)

Why use LinkedIn to market you and/or your business

LinkedIn differs from other social media platforms because it is focused primarily on business. Certainly, you will come across posts on the platform more suited to Facebook or Instagram, but by and large, LinkedIn users post business or work-related content and connect to others for work-related purposes.

The behaviour exhibited on LinkedIn is generally of a higher standard than seen on other platforms. Trolling, inappropriate messages and other abusive behaviours are not common. True, there are those who have had a bad experience, but by and large most LinkedIn users find it a positive environment in which to communicate.

The number of publishing options available on LinkedIn also makes it different from other platforms. You can choose from text posts, long form articles, images, images plus text, documents (Word, PDF, slide shows), native video, video on other platforms (e.g. YouTube), polls, website links and, by the time you read this, probably others. Some of these can be added to profiles, while others can be published as posts or included in articles.

Another of LinkedIn's points of difference is the ability to find what you're looking for right there on the platform. Whether that's the latest information on artificial intelligence, a new form of personality testing in recruitment, how to be a podcast guest or something else entirely, you don't have to leave LinkedIn to find it. LinkedIn is a platform on which to share content that will build your reputation, credibility and standing.

The 4 Link·Ability strategies

Making clever use of four elements of LinkedIn – connecting, publishing, engaging and direct messaging – either individually or in various combinations will enable you to achieve your professional goals or objectives.

Connecting: I detail the right and wrong ways to extend your network so you are connecting with those who may potentially become clients or be advantageous to you in other ways. Who you connect to and how you connect is far more important than connecting to huge numbers of people who may or may not have an interest in you and your work. Many people will connect with just anyone, but I advocate targeting connections using the parameters LinkedIn provides so you become connected with the right people.

Publishing: I cover all the existing options for posting, revealing what is best practice and how to get the most from your content. LinkedIn offers a multitude of formats for publishing posts and articles which can achieve wide organic reach. Publishing on LinkedIn is one of the best opportunities online to showcase your knowledge and skills because relatively few people do it, and even fewer do it well.

Engaging: I explain how to engage in a way that adds value to conversations so you stand out for all the right reasons. A stand-alone strategy that has been proven to work, engaging is the simple act of commenting on and sharing other people's posts. Done consistently, this can be very effective but relies on having a good-sized network of targeted connections to provide sufficient content. This is ideal for those who don't wish to or can't create their own content on a regular basis but still want their name to be seen in the newsfeed.

Direct messaging: I discuss the significant advantages that LinkedIn messaging has over email. One of them is that your message is placed directly in front of the person you're aiming at and they will receive a notification. There are right and wrong ways to do this however, but when done correctly, it generates enquiry. Direct messaging is not the place for spamming people so my discussion includes how to avoid the pitfalls and send messages that will resonate, build trust and develop relationships.

Leveraging the strategies for success

Throughout this book I tackle each of the strategies mentioned above and discuss how to combine them to leverage the power of LinkedIn. I provide examples so you can see how they have worked – or failed – to help you decide which will work for you, too. I've also provided a 'quick reference' list on the back of each chapter page, to help you quickly and easily find what you are looking for. You can keep this book handy as a reference while you are working on LinkedIn.

By learning how each of these strategies work, you can then decide which is best when matching your objectives against the resources available to you. Over time, you will see what's working and what isn't. You can then drop the strategies that don't deliver and concentrate on those that do.

LinkedIn's unique features make it the perfect social media platform for business. If you are keen to develop professionally, generate leads or stand out in a positive way, LinkedIn is the place to be. By using the four strategies I discuss in this book and developing a plan to use them in your LinkedIn marketing, you will gain visibility, credibility and professional recognition. Connect to the right people and develop meaningful relationships with them by consistent and diligent sharing of content, and the opportunities you seek, and even ones you hadn't thought of, will come your way.

If you are keen to make skilful use of LinkedIn to achieve your professional ambitions, I invite you to learn more in the chapters ahead.

Connecting

The heart of the LinkedIn engine

In this chapter:

THE FIRST LinkedIn activity you must do when you have created a top-notch profile (which you can find out how to do at wordwizard.co.nz/book-resources) is to invite people to connect with you. You will probably have two immediate responses to the idea of connecting:

1. Connect with anybody and everybody, by hitting the Connect button OR

2. Only connect with people you know personally, and even then tentatively in case they think you're being too pushy or commercial.

Levels of connection

On Facebook people who want to hear from each other are called **friends**, on LinkedIn they are **connections**. LinkedIn has three levels of connection – 1st-, 2nd- and 3rd-degree.

Those who are **1st-degree connections** have agreed to be connected to each other. They see each other's posts in their newsfeeds and are able to message each other directly.

Those who are **2nd-degree connections** are not directly connected, but have at least one 1st-degree connection in common.

A **3rd-degree connection** is someone with whom you have at least one 2nd-degree connection in common.

The term **network** is used in this book to collectively mean 1st-degree connections.

Connecting as a strategy

Connecting is a strategy that you need to consider carefully before deciding the best approach to take. For instance, you need to decide what your objective for connecting is and then ensure your actions actively work towards your outcomes. For example, if you want to build your reputation as someone who knows the industry inside out, you will want to connect with other industry experts so you can learn from and develop a relationship with them and become part of that community. Entrepreneur, author and motivational speaker Jim Rohn once said,

'We are the average of the five people we spend the most time with.'

While it might not be quite so literally accurate on LinkedIn, the sentiment certainly holds true.

You want to be connected with people who will lift you up and guide, teach and support you. Positive people whom you admire, whether they are in your industry or not. The more of these kinds of people you connect and engage with, the more of them you will find. As a collaborative platform, LinkedIn has one of the best networks of people like you who want to make a difference. That's one of the reasons it is such an exciting and empowering platform to be on.

Building a strong, engaged network

Building a strong network of high-quality connections is critical to mastering LinkedIn. What does this mean for you? It means connecting and engaging with someone who has a large number of connections or followers (in the thousands for preference) and a fully complete profile with plenty of detail, including a professional photograph of themselves.

A high-quality connection is also someone who is active on LinkedIn by posting useful content regularly and engaging with others' posts. The more people like this in your network, the greater the chances that the material you post will be seen by a large audience.

If your connections have few connections and are not active on LinkedIn few people will see or engage with your posts and your efforts will be in vain.

A surprising number of LinkedIn members do not actively seek out new connections and therefore have only a small network and a correspondingly small footprint on the platform. They see LinkedIn as the online version of their CV. They focus on themselves, how great they are, their achievements and performance. They don't *get* LinkedIn. LinkedIn is about creating new connections by sharing knowledge and insights, about engaging with connections in a genuine and meaningful way, about NOT SELLING you. It's about genuine interest and realtionship building. Of course, this may well lead to a new client/customer, but engage meaningfully first, build trust and mean it.

As of writing, LinkedIn shows the number of connections a person has on the introduction to their profile if it is under 500, as in the example over the page.

If a profile has over 500 **connections**, the introduction section merely says '500+ connections'. The number of **followers** they have (note the distinction) is displayed in the Activity section, as seen in the screenshot over the page. While connections are people directly connected through an invitation having been extended and accepted, followers are those who follow someone's activity without necessarily being connected to them. However, by default, connections are automatically followers, too, although this can be changed.

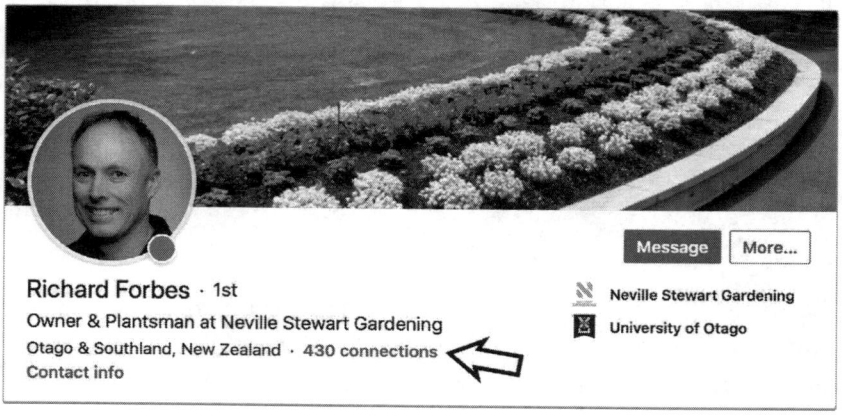

A LinkedIn profile with under 500 connections.

A profile with 8,281 followers. Note that this number is likely to differ from the number of connections a person has.

How many connections do you need?

It is commonly considered that 500 is the minimum number of 1st-degree connections you need for a viable, credible profile, although for LinkedIn marketing, your connections will need to number in the thousands. Just how many thousands is dependent on your industry, what you are trying to achieve on LinkedIn and the time or resources you have available to send connection invite messages (more on that later). A good way to determine the right ballpark to be in is to look at the follower numbers of those in your industry at your own level and those above or where you aspire to be.

If you are thoughtful with your connecting strategy, it will take months or even years to build a network of targeted connections so don't be discouraged if your numbers don't increase very quickly. Spend 15 minutes a day searching for people to connect to and sending personalised messages, and watch your network build. (More coming up on the best way to do this.)

But it isn't just all about the numbers. What's paramount is the relationship you build with those connections. Because even if a LinkedIn member has agreed to become a connection, it doesn't mean they will necessarily be open to communicating with you directly, especially at first. You will need to cement your relationship by building trust.

When meeting anyone new for the first time, online or off, HOW you begin the relationship is key. I remember several years ago being introduced to a rather important man at a networking event. He didn't look me in the eye as the introduction was made, instead his gaze was concentrated considerably lower than my face, and despite my wearing a name tag positioned exactly where he was staring, he made no effort to get my name right. As soon as I was introduced, he moved on without even attempting the usual pleasantries. The person introducing me had no opportunity to explain why she wanted him to meet me, which was because I was editor of an industry publication and interested in publishing a feature about him and his company. Not all people are so blatantly rude when you meet them (and so miss these opportunities) but you certainly don't forget them!

On LinkedIn, the etiquette isn't quite as clear cut. For instance, on its Connections Overview page LinkedIn says, 'The basic type of connection is a contact you know personally and who you trust on a professional level.' In reality, it is not necessary to know someone personally before connecting with them and LinkedIn encourages connecting more widely.

Most people now consider it perfectly acceptable to invite and be invited to connect by people they don't yet know. Only a few still cling to the outdated belief that they need to personally know the person before connecting. There are also some who will connect only with people who are in close geographic proximity or the same industry. The main thing when inviting someone to connect is to be clear about why you are asking so they can see if it will be worthwhile for them. However, most active LinkedIn users are willing, interested and happy to connect.

One of LinkedIn's greatest opportunities lies in those people you don't know but may wish to. These could be industry leaders, peers, potential clients, people you could learn from and those in fields you are interested in but are not directly involved with. I have 'met' on LinkedIn many people I would never have the opportunity to meet in person but who have enriched my life in different ways. There was the New Zealander of the Year who sent me a copy of his riveting memoir, the UK podcast host who interviewed me for his international show, the US LinkedIn trainer who has become a friend with whom I share LinkedIn ideas, the Queensland social entrepreneur who set me up with my first virtual assistants, and those I interact with who continue to give me ideas and teach me lessons I didn't know I needed to learn.

LinkedIn in Action

The owner of a specialised learning company wanted her students to understand the importance of a strong LinkedIn profile. They were young women who ultimately wanted to work in the science and health industries.

The business owner had received many lifechanging opportunities and understood the value of a large, engaged network. She instilled in her students the necessity to start early with their LinkedIn profiles so they could develop connections that would stand them in good stead in the years ahead.

She encouraged her students to connect with people they may have been inspired by – industry leaders they could meet virtually and learn from, and perhaps find a way to relate to more personally, cementing a longer term relationship. Despite their initial reluctance, many of the students took their courage in both hands and began networking through LinkedIn, beginning relationships that, if nurtured, could help them in their careers.

· · ·

The CEO of a business association saw no value in connecting on LinkedIn with her members and so had masses of connection invites backed up. This inadvertently sent the message to members that she didn't care enough to connect with them.

But while attending a conference she heard from her international counterparts how they were using LinkedIn to not only communicate with and add value for existing members but to attract potential new members. She had an ah-ha moment as she realised how she could use LinkedIn as a low-cost method to recruit new members.

Once back at her desk after the conference, the CEO cleared her backlog of invites, sending an apology message for the delay in accepting. She also actively began sending invites to her membership database so she would have a strong network of engaged members who could help her recruitment efforts.

Having a large network of people from all corners of the globe is an exciting prospect but there is a potential downside as noted by my LinkedIn trainer friend in the USA, JoAnne Funch. In her blog (bit.ly/2TiGeQT), she says, 'LinkedIn decides (or the algorithm decides) which of your connections will see your content. Why take the chance that the wrong people are seeing what you post versus people you want to influence when you post.' This is an excellent argument for ensuring the people you connect with are the right people for your purposes. If, for instance, you want to bring in leads to your business, then connecting with potential clients is a better strategy than connecting with your own industry peers.

So, too, if you want to be seen as an expert in your field. You will want those who can benefit from your expertise to be in your network rather than those who are already at the level you are aspiring to. Instead of connecting, follow these people if you want to see what they are posting.

All the experts agree – you are better to have closer relationships with a smaller number of connections than to have thousands of connections whom you hardly or don't know.

But what do you do if you have already amassed a large network of people who are virtually unknown to you? Well, you have some work to do and here's the best advice I can offer you on this:

- Go through your connections and decide who you want to build a relationship with. This might be based on how well you knew them in the past, their current role or their potential as a client. It might simply be because you like them!

- Look at their LinkedIn profile so they can see you are interested in them. You will also learn potentially useful information about them.

- Make contact however you feel comfortable – LinkedIn direct message (DM), email, phone – and start a conversation. Know what you want to say before you begin if you're calling. But it could be as simple as, "You and I haven't been in touch for a while and I wanted just to reach out, say hello, and ask how you are." Be honest, authentic and yourself.

Build or rebuild your relationship with your connection in a way that shows you genuinely care. If you don't genuinely care, don't. People will see right through you. For connections whom you do not wish to contact personally ask yourself, 'Why am I connected?' If being connected has value to you, keep them. If not, consider unconnecting.

Before you begin connecting

As with all of the strategies discussed in this book, there is a baseline you need to be at before you begin connecting. You will need an All Star LinkedIn profile with all sections completed to best practice level. If you are unsure what this means, I have an e-book on the topic available at wordwizard.co.nz/book-resources. This will help you update or upgrade your profile to represent your experience and skills professionally and clearly so you stand out from your competitors or peers. There is, after all, no point in asking people to connect with you when your profile is inadequate, out of date or just generally poor. They will be reluctant to connect unless they see a pressing need such as a company policy that states all members of the organisation must connect with each other. Even then, you don't want to make a poor impression with a miserable excuse for a LinkedIn profile. Anyone thinking of doing business with you will check out your LinkedIn profile at some point in their buying process.

Never *ever* forget that when someone Googles your name, one of the first search results that comes up will be your LinkedIn profile.

Here's a reminder of some of the most important aspects of a LinkedIn profile which should be completed or uploaded before you begin connecting. You need:

- A professional head and shoulders profile photograph (not a happy snap from your latest holiday or one taken with selfie stick in your office). Smile, show some teeth!

- A unique cover or header image (also known as the background photograph), that sits at the top of your profile. For the best ways to create a cover image visit wordwizard.co.nz/book-resources.

- A completed About section that tells the story and journey of your professional life.

- A number of eye-catching thumbnails in the Featured section (previously part of the About section).

- A personal LinkedIn URL (as opposed to the default one LinkedIn gives you that ends in a bunch of random numbers).

- Completed and up-to-date contact information including listing three web pages relevant to your work.

- A 220-character Headline that succinctly describes what you do, for whom and the benefits.

- An Experience section that lists and provides details of all recent and relevant jobs.

- A comprehensive list of your skills for Endorsements.

- A minimum of five Recommendations.

Why connecting is *so* important

Connecting with the right people on LinkedIn can change your life in ways you might not have imagined. It can bring in business (especially when combined with the other strategies in this book) and deliver opportunities you may not even have considered. For example:

- It could bring you to the attention of a podcast host who may decide to interview you.

- You might be asked to join a board because of your expertise in governance.

- You might be offered an interview with a leading journalist or writer.

- You could be invited to give a keynote address at a prestigious industry conference, or

- You might meet people who open new doors for you. Because, remember, we all like to do business with those we know, like and trust. And nowhere online can you do that more easily, quickly or better than on LinkedIn.

As important as connecting is, even more crucial is the strategy you adopt when connecting. By this I mean WHO you decide to connect with. Is it your potential customers, industry peers or leaders, the people in your immediate network or a combination of all these plus perhaps some other categories such as fellow university graduates? When starting out on LinkedIn, most people connect first with people they know. Once that list is exhausted, they start to think about who else they might like to have in their network.

Finding the *right* LinkedIn connections

There is a right way to begin a LinkedIn relationship and connecting is where it starts. Get this right and everything else will fall into place.

LinkedIn is a great place to research potential connections. There are several ways to search. You can do so through the:

- My Network page.
- The Search box.
- LinkedIn's paid Sales Navigator or Premium accounts.
- Syncing your email contacts.

My Network page

If you have a free LinkedIn account (and it's all you need when starting out) the best place to find suggestions for new connections is on the **My Network** page. LinkedIn will also suggest Groups, Pages, Hashtags and Newsletters to follow. When you hit the Connect button below the person's profile overview an invitation is sent, and that person will be replaced by a new suggestion. Two words of warning about this though.

First, on free accounts there is a ceiling on the number of invites you can send via this page before LinkedIn will prompt you to move to a paid account.

Second, you will not be able to personalise the message you send (see the importance of personalisation and how to go about it on page 26). This reduces the likelihood of someone who doesn't know you and hasn't heard of you accepting your connection invite. The way around this is to:

- Go to the person's profile.

- Connect with them by clicking on the Connect button under their cover image.

- This opens a new page containing a box in which you can write a personal message.

The added benefit of this is that they will be able to see you have visited their profile which counts in your favour when they are deciding whether to hit the Accept or Ignore button.

In addition to inviting other members to connect with you from the My Network page, you can connect with someone from wherever you happen to spot their profile photograph. Click on their photograph and you will be taken directly to their profile where you can connect with them, writing your own message if you wish to. One of the great things about LinkedIn is that your profile image (and the first few words of your headline) follow you around so that the more you're seen out and about on the platform, the easier it is for people to connect with you.

Search box

The second place to go to find potential new connections is the **Search box** at the top of any LinkedIn page. You can use this for searching for companies, content, schools, groups and jobs. LinkedIn is a very powerful search engine in its own right, much like Google, particularly for searching for new connections.

Say, for example, you want to connect with marketing managers from other local companies. You would:

- Click on People.

- Choose from the filters available that include Locations and Current Companies.

All Filters will bring up a wider range of options.

LinkedIn paid accounts

The third place for finding people to connect with is through LinkedIn's paid account options. Two of these are **LinkedIn Premium** and **Sales Navigator**. The latter is a much more comprehensive version of the former and by extension, more expensive. Sales Navigator has enhanced search capability and the ability to save searches. For a discussion on the merits of free versus paid accounts, listen to the podcast LinkedInformed.com/episode237 with Mr LinkedIn, Mark Williams.

Deciding whether to connect

Once you have located a potential connection, the decision to make is whether you should actually connect with them. Here's what to consider.

1. **Number of connections.** If they have only a few connections it likely means they aren't a regular LinkedIn user. They may not see your connection invite message, much less bother replying. It is not uncommon for infrequent users to have dozens of outstanding connection requests. This is worth keeping in mind if you are planning to use LinkedIn for publishing posts and articles. If your connections have only a few 1st-degree

connections each your network won't be big enough for your material to be seen by a large audience.

2. **Profile image.** If you don't know your potential connection personally, you will want to see what they look like! Rightly or wrongly, this helps you decide if you want to be connected with them. If there is no profile image or it is poor you might want to reconsider your connection request. See my ebook at wordwizard.co.nz/book-resources for what constitutes an optimal profile image.

3. **Quality of their profile.** Is it complete, with plenty of detail and media? Or is it a bare bones effort which again might lead you to conclude that the person is not a frequent user of LinkedIn and is unlikely to be a good connection for you?

4. **Activity on LinkedIn.** Do they post regularly or engage with others' posts often? If they do, they might deserve to be part of your network. But do not judge solely on this as many people take no part in the day-to-day activities of the platform or its members, and are content to watch from the sidelines. You will not know they are taking any notice of you until they get in touch out of the blue and say, 'I've been following your activity on LinkedIn.' This happens more regularly than you might imagine so consider it along with those mentioned above.

The best people to connect with are those who regularly visit and spend time on the platform. That way they'll spot your material in the newsfeed, see notifications about your activity and may even run searches in which you appear. In all, they are better prospects for your LinkedIn efforts and are what you should be concentrating on. This is not to say that people with poor profiles, few connections and little if any activity will not be good prospects for your business. They may be. But they may not spend much time on LinkedIn and if this is where you are putting your marketing efforts, you want the right people to see and take note.

The critical element of connection – personalisation

Like any good relationship, a LinkedIn relationship is two-way. Anyone you want to connect with must give their permission and they do so by agreeing to your connection request. The alternatives are for you to follow the person rather than connect, as explained earlier, and to engage with their posts in the hope they will extend an invitation to you. This does happen from time to time.

Persuading that person to connect is therefore very important. The most effective way to do this is through a personalised connection request/message. Sending no message at all is tantamount to asking to have your invitation ignored, although it happens constantly, usually from people who have no wish to engage in a reciprocal relationship, merely sell to you. I know of a company director who spends his daily commute with his head buried in his phone, hitting the Connect button on the People You May Know page again and again. He is not particular about who he connects with, he invites everyone LinkedIn suggests. It's like using a net, dragging in everyone regardless of whether they are appropriate connections or not. And because he has the title 'director' in his profile, he has a higher rate of acceptance than the rest of us might achieve. However, the folly of this technique is obvious when looking at the engagement he receives on his posts. Virtually none – and very few views either. He is not connecting to the right people.

When sending a personalised message it must answer the question that is uppermost in your potential connection's mind if they don't know you personally – why are you asking me? Why, indeed!

You should not start by pitching them your product or service – selling to them – and hoping they will buy from you. This is not a good way to begin. Start by developing a relationship where you can add value through sharing your knowledge and expertise; the sale can come later.

In order to persuade others to connect with you, you need to be clear on your objective – what you want from this relationship. Are you interested in the subjects they post about? Are you intending to develop a professional relationship with them or do you want them in your network so you can share value over time, nurturing them as a potential lead? How important to you is it that the person accepts? If you are very keen to have them in your network, you will want to put more work into persuading them to say yes.

Types of connection invite messages

There are three kinds of connection invites.

1. No message.

2. A personalised message (referencing them by name) that is somewhat generic in that it can be sent to almost anyone.

3. A message personalised to the particular person that is very obviously tailored for them.

1. No message

Sending no message at all is the laziest, lowest value type of connection message you can send and therefore receives the least response. People who are merely collecting members to build a large network do this but generally end up with a motley collection of potentially irrelevant connections who they have no personal interest in or relationship with. And given that the LinkedIn algorithm makes decisions on what it places in your newsfeed partly based on who you are connected to, connecting indiscriminately will likely result in yours being filled with irrelevant and uninteresting posts.

2. Personalised but generic message

Sending a personalised but semi-generic message is used by those who want potential connections to take notice of them and accept their invite. They may be sending these in large numbers albeit within the confines of LinkedIn's rules.

It is generally understood that LinkedIn allows each member to send 75 invites a day, each up to 300 characters long. Send more and there is a danger that LinkedIn could see this as a violation of their terms of service and take your account down. This is no idle threat; LinkedIn can and will close your account if they are not happy with your activities. It is quite a mission to get it back!

A personal but semi-generic message might look like this:

Hello [first name]

LinkedIn is such a great way to connect with people you might not ordinarily have a chance to meet and as you and I already have connections in common – including [name] – I wondered if you would care to connect?

Or this:

Hello [name]

I'm gradually increasing my presence on LinkedIn and am reaching out to other business professionals so I wondered if you'd like to connect?

In the first message, you're establishing your credibility by pointing out that you're connected to people they may know. In the second, you're again establishing credibility but this time as a business professional. You're saying, for example, that you're not just anyone off the street, you're someone with standing in the business world.

It is worth noting that not all devices behave the same way. For instance, it's a little more fiddly to send a personalised invite by mobile.

3. Personalised and tailored message

The third message type – tailored to the recipient – requires some work on your part before you can send it. Start by visiting their profile. Find something you have in common with that person – you went to the same university, worked at the same company, have a mutual friend or something about their profile appeals to you such as their headline, cover image, a video – you can comment on. You can also look at and/or comment on some of their articles and posts. The key is to demonstrate you have been to their profile and spent time looking at it. Provided the person isn't super-strict about their connections, you are almost always guaranteed an acceptance with this approach. The downside is that it takes time so I would advocate a combination of 2 and 3 above if you are aiming to increase your connection numbers at a reasonable rate. I never send an invite without a message unless I have previously arranged with the person to invite them, but even then it feels rude not to add a personal note.

What to do once you have connected

For many people, the main aim of connecting is to collect names in order to increase the size of their network. After connecting, no messages are exchanged and neither bothers to engage with each other's posts or articles. This is not the best use of LinkedIn. Nor does it much advance any potential relationship that could lead to business or other opportunities.

Connecting is just the first step. Second is the follow-up.

Most people don't bother with this step, yet I believe it is one of the most important. What follows the agreement to connect may determine the fate of the entire relationship so it is worth spending a minute or two responding. After all, if it was worth connecting in the first place, it must surely be worth your time to acknowledge that connection.

It is. And the results will be worth it if you do it well because, once again, you'll stand out. You've already shown yourself to be different from 90% of other LinkedIn members by sending a personalised invite. Now cement that difference with a well-worded follow-up message.

There are three main ways to do this – by sending a written, voice or video message.

1. Written message

Of the three, a written message is the quickest and easiest. It is also the least effective. You can write a thank you message from desktop or mobile which means it's a task that can be done between other more pressing matters or while you're waiting for your next meeting to start. (If you are unsure about direct messaging on LinkedIn and how to do it, there is a full explanation at the beginning of the Direct Messaging chapter.)

A written message needn't be long. In fact, it shouldn't be otherwise you run the risk of your new connection thinking you're trying to sell or spam them. The effect you are trying to create is for them to FEEL good about the fact they've received this message from you, not apprehensive that it might be pressure of some kind. After all, if you are going to base your relationship with them on sharing valuable information and material, they need to know they can trust you. Or at least, begin to build that trust. As we know, trust – like reputation – can take time to build, but only moments to destroy. Don't demolish it at the very beginning by using the wrong approach.

A short, succinct message is all that's needed at this stage. Here's one I commonly use:

> 'Thank you for accepting my invitation. It's great to be connected and I look forward to learning more about you and your work over the coming months.'

It's generic and can be used in pretty much most circumstances. If you want to make an even greater impression, say something like:

> 'Thanks so much for accepting my LinkedIn connection invite, [name]. I'm glad to be part of your network now and hope to learn more about the [industry] from you via your posts and activity on the newsfeed in the coming months.'

Or:

> 'Thanks for connecting, [name]. I see we both know [name]. In fact, I went to school with him. How do you know him?'

A question is an excellent way to get the conversational ball rolling, and if your new connection feels compelled to answer, a conversation has begun. If, however, your connection doesn't personally know the person you have mentioned, they will be less inclined to respond. Take the strongest common thread you have with the person and use that. If you attended the same university, once lived in the same city or at one time worked for the same organisation, use that as your conversational leverage.

However you approach written follow-up messages, the trick is to have your most commonly used ones saved within easy copying distance, such as on a Sticky on your desktop, where you can easily grab it and insert it into LinkedIn's message function. On mobile, you could save it in Notes.

2. Voice message

The second of the three follow-up message options is my preferred method – voice messages. Few people use it so you stand out when you send the message, and the response is often surprise (*'I didn't know you could do this on LinkedIn'*) and pleasure that you have taken the time to send the message.

In a world where few leave phone voice messages anymore, LinkedIn voice messages have a novelty value that gives them more kudos than a simple phone message would have. Of course, this supposes that your message is as similarly non-threatening as the written message examples above.

Voice messages can be sent from the mobile app only; as of the first half of 2020 they were not available on desktop. They are simple to use and can be up to one minute long. If you don't like what you've recorded, delete it and start again.

My husband, Matthew Mewse, The Telephone Man, advises having three different messages prepared and in front of you when recording. He says that if you use the same one consistently it begins to sound forced when the effect you're looking for is that it's special to that particular person. He also says that using the same message continually can result in it sounding a bit sing-song, or worse, monotonous. I get round this by emphasising different words or phrases each time so it doesn't sound the same. Or, if there's something I've noticed about the person's profile I can comment on then I often insert that, too.

Here's my usual voice message:

> *'Hi [name]. This is Lynnaire Johnston, the Word Wizard. Just a very quick message to say thank you so much for accepting my invite to connect here on LinkedIn. I'm very pleased to be part of your network now and I look forward to learning more about you and your work through your posts and activity on the newsfeed over the coming months. Thanks again for connecting, [name]. Bye for now.'*

I make sure upfront that they know they're not receiving a long message which might put them off. Usually mine are 20–25 seconds. As well, I use their name twice – at the beginning and end – and my name only once.

As with written messages, if I notice something on their profile that's worthy of comment – their header image for instance – I'll mention that. But only something positive. I never, ever tell them that their profile needs improvement in any way.

3. Video message

The third type of messaging you might like to try is video. You will REALLY stand out with this (I've only ever received a handful) but if your message is to be personalised for your new connection, there's a time factor involved and a danger.

There are plenty of free programs for quickly and easily recording videos, including the LinkedIn mobile app, allowing you to upload them in a timely fashion. That's the good news. The bad news is that with video, your new connection can see you (duh!) so you need to work harder to make a good impression and to come across as professional. Record a personalised video from your phone via the messaging section of the LinkedIn mobile app and you run the risk of bad lighting, poor sound and your double chins being visible. Conversely, recording a generic message that is sent to every new connection robs you of the advantage of being personal. Everyone responds differently, but it's personalisation that's important at this stage in the relationship. You can always send a generic video message later on.

My suggestion for any first video is to keep it short, smile a lot and make the person feel welcome. As with written and voice messages, thank them for connecting, mention you're glad to be part of their network, compliment them on, or mention something from their profile and keep it low-key and non-salesy.

The aim of the exercise is to make a good impression, so look and sound professional, and film the video in a business setting – not sitting on the beach enjoying a cocktail (unless, of course, this is where you conduct business). If your phone doesn't have this feature, it's time you upgraded. Take it from someone who knows, the longer you leave technology upgrades the harder it is to get to grips with the new innovations.

One of my strongest LinkedIn connection relationships is with the US-based LinkedIn trainer JoAnne Funch I mentioned earlier in this chapter. It began with her sending me a video message. I was super-impressed and our relationship has gone from strength to strength. Imagine if you could do that with a potential client! Whatever method you decide on, connection follow-up messages are an important part of breaking through on LinkedIn.

Receiving connection invites

I love finding invitations from potential new connections in my LinkedIn inbox especially when someone has made the effort to send me a personal message. Most invites are not personalised so when they are I like to take time to look at the inviter's profile. That way I feel I know a little about them.

Developing a set of parameters for deciding who to accept will help you build a targeted network. These might include the industry they work in, where they are located and whether they are active on LinkedIn.

If I have any doubts at all about a person who has sent me an invitation, I don't connect. For example, take a connection invite I received recently. The inviter had only a few connections, his head was mostly out of shot in his profile photograph and he had no cover image. As well, his profile was virtually empty and what he did have was marked 'confidential'. Plus, his industry didn't interest me, either as a potential client or someone to buy from. I suspected this was a bogus account and not a real person at all so I declined his non-personalised invitation to connect.

But in cases where I do accept a connection invitation I will follow up with a voice message, just as if I'd invited them to connect. Even if there's no personal message in their invite. I want them to know that I will be communicating with them further down the track and although I don't say this in my message, the fact that I've messaged at all indicates that they're likely to be hearing from me in the future.

The benefits of connecting strategically

Connecting is at the heart of winning with LinkedIn and if you plan to use the platform in a strategic way to achieve your business goals, it is essential. Without a strong network of relevant, well-placed people with whom you have built or are in the process of building solid relationships, any other strategies discussed in this book will fail.

All these strategies start with connections. Surround yourself on LinkedIn with like-minded professionals who can help you move forward just as you, by your own activities on the platform such as sharing useful information, help others.

Developing a strategy for your connecting activities is the key to making this part of your LinkedIn plan successful. Critical questions to ask include:

- What parameters will you use to decide on those you choose to connect with? These might include how many connections they have, whether there is a professional photograph and a completed profile, and if they are active on the platform.

- If you're serious about LinkedIn, should you purchase a paid account and if so, which one?

- How will you choose who to connect to? By inviting whoever LinkedIn recommends or by targeting people you feel will be the right fit?

- How much time can you put into sending invites each day?

- Will your invites be personalised or generic?

- Will you follow up with a written, voice or video message to get the ball rolling and attempt to develop a profesional relationship?

The answers to these questions will come from knowing what it is you want to achieve from LinkedIn. If, for example, you want to be known widely and have high visibility, you might opt for increasing your connection numbers as fast as possible as opposed to developing relationships. But if you want to get to know the top people in your industry, a more personal, highly targeted approach will be necessary. Consider what you want to achieve and work accordingly. This table will help you decide.

Objective	Tactics						
	Connect widely	Connect with targeted LinkedIn members	Generic invitations	Personal invitations	Use free account	Purchase paid account	Send follow-up message
Become known as an expert	✓			✓		✓	✓
Increase visibility	✓		✓		✓		✓
Bring in business		✓		✓		✓	✓
Industry recognition		✓		✓	✓		✓
Learn from the best in the world	✓	✓		✓			✓
Gain media opportunities				✓	✓		✓

Top tips for connecting

1. Have a reason for connecting.

Don't connect with just anyone and everyone. Have a solid reason for asking another LinkedIn member to connect with you. Perhaps you know or have met them, they're a potential client or supplier, or you could learn from them because they're industry leaders.

2. View someone's profile before inviting them to connect.

This increases the likelihood of their accepting and also ensures you know something about them and can be sure you want to connect. Random connecting is not considered best practice.

3. Choose parameters for invitees.

If someone has no profile photograph and an incomplete profile, they're probably not spending much time on the platform and so won't see your posts or messages. Likewise if they have only a few connections and there is little or nothing showing in the Activity area on their profile.

4. Never send an invitation without a message.

Take the time to send a personalised message of invitation if you want someone to accept. The chances of a yes are much greater if you have explained why you want to connect, mentioned a connection in common or shown that you've visited their profile.

5. Always follow up with a thank you.

If someone has agreed to connect with you it is only polite that you acknowledge this with a thank you. It can also open the door to a discussion or opportunity if you make it sufficiently personal. Voice messages make great thank you messages.

6. Never spam a new connection.

A LinkedIn connection is about building a relationship, not touting for business. Connecting to someone simply to sell to them is a mistake and your connection will most likely react badly unless you just happen to be offering the very thing they are looking for at that very moment. The chances of that are slim.

7. Check out the profiles of people who invite you to connect.

While LinkedIn is a much safer social media environment than other platforms, not everything or everyone is necessarily as they seem. Never feel obliged to connect to someone if you feel uncomfortable about doing so.

8. Follow instead of connecting.

If you want to see what a competitor is doing on LinkedIn but don't want them to know you're looking, follow them instead of connecting with them. Their activity will show up in your notifications.

9. Engage with new connections (Like, Comment and Share).

Once you have connected with someone, make sure you engage with the posts and articles they upload to LinkedIn. (More on this in Chapter 3, Engaging.) This shows true interest in them and their business which will help to build the relationship.

Summary

Whether used in isolation, or in conjunction with other strategies, connecting with other LinkedIn members is a game changer that can make a big difference to your success. Spend even a few minutes a day to search out potential new connections, invite them in a personal and friendly way, and you will soon reap the rewards.

Decide on your objectives first so you can map out your approach before starting (you can always change tack later). Once you have connected, make sure to keep the conversation going to really establish the relationship. Your invitees might be very popular and receive many requests to connect. Stand out in your approach and follow up, and they will be more likely to remember who you are and what you do. Keep in touch, don't let the relationship languish and you have a recipe for Link·Ability.

Checklists

Connecting process

Decide on the right type of potential connections for your purposes.
Locate their names through searches.
Look at their profiles to check they meet your parameters.
Send each potential connection a personalised invitation.
When you are notified of a new connection, follow up with a written, voice or video message
Send no more than 75 connection invites a day.

Connection invite and thank you follow-up message ideas

Generic connection invite	Your name popped up in a search I was doing today and I thought it too good an opportunity not to get in touch and suggest that we connect.
Generic connection invite	I'm gradually increasing my presence on LinkedIn and am reaching out to other business professionals, so I wondered if you'd like to connect?
Generic connection invite	Your name came up in my LinkedIn feed recently, and as we have connections in common, I wondered if you would care to connect?
Industry specific invite	I've recently been working with [industry name] professionals and [name something you have in common], so because of that link I wondered if you'd like to connect.
When someone has reacted to one of your published posts	Hello – recently you kindly interacted on a post I published here on LinkedIn. Thanks so much for taking part. I wonder if you would care to connect?
When someone has looked at your profile but not connected with you	Hello – I see you've recently popped by my profile and now I've visited yours, so I wondered if you would care to connect?
When someone has accepted your invitation to connect	Thank you for accepting my invitation. It's great to be connected and I'll look forward to learning more about you and your work over the coming months.
Generic thank you for connecting message	Hello and thanks so much for connecting with me. It's great to be part of your network and I'm looking forward to learning more about what you do via the newsfeed.

Publishing

The power of posting content on LinkedIn

In this chapter:

Why post on LinkedIn?

LinkedIn provides a publishing platform that makes it possible for any business professional in any line of work to get their name and that of their business noticed. Noticed by potential clients, employers, suppliers, advisors, collaborators and more. In many senses, LinkedIn is a level playing field where anyone can post content others will read, even those who are not confident writers, and it is cost-free to do so.

This visibility will help you achieve the objectives you identified in the introduction to this book, whether that is to build personal brand recognition, bring leads into your business, promote yourself and/or your company, become known as an expert in your field or learn from others.

These numbers from LinkedIn explain why:

- The LinkedIn feed attracts 9 billion content impressions every week, making it an ideal place to share content. (**Impressions** are the total number of times content is made available to users so is the maximum number of times it could have been seen. It should not be confused with **reach** which is the total number of people who see the content.)

- Only 3 million users share content weekly – not many for the large number of people looking for quality content. The platform is massively under-utilised, which provides myriad opportunities for those alert to the benefits.

- LinkedIn is the top place to find quality content according to 91% of marketing executives. Other social media platforms are down in the twenties.

- Views of material published in the LinkedIn newsfeed increase exponentially each year.

- Engagement is booming with comments, likes, and shares increasing 60% year-on-year and indications are that this has skyrocketed in 2020.

- Nearly half (45%) of social media traffic to a company's home page comes from LinkedIn.

- Nearly half (45%) of LinkedIn article readers are in senior positions, making them decision-makers.

It might seem that the LinkedIn newsfeed is so crowded there is no opportunity left to stamp your mark. Yet, the facts don't bear this out. There is still a huge chunk of the LinkedIn membership not utilising the platform as well as they might. And that represents a golden opportunity for you, your brand and your company.

The report *State of Digital Selling with LinkedIn 2019* by respected American digital sales organisation Vengreso found that more than a third of LinkedIn members (39%) never share content on their LinkedIn network and only 16% share several times a week. It goes on to contend that this is a major missed chance given that companies using editorial content as part of their sales strategy have a higher sales win rate than those which don't. Further, more than 80% of buyers consume five or more articles or pieces of content from the vendor they ultimately select to provide the product or service they choose to buy. So, while those pieces of content could be published in a variety of places, if a company isn't also sharing content on LinkedIn, their chances of securing a sale are reduced. Now, if your average sale price is $5.50, producing content on LinkedIn probably isn't worth the effort unless you sell bucket loads to business professionals. But if high ticket items are your game or the lifetime sales value of a client is considerable, then ignoring LinkedIn is indeed a major missed opportunity.

Tamara Schenk, research director of CSO Insights, a sales research and data organisation, says that **engaging buyers successfully** via social media requires valuable, relevant and differentiating content. To do that requires a strategy that offers tailored content and an integrated social selling approach. Whether it's a relevant article, report, presentation or a video, it is crucial to consistently publish updates and share content to your network to earn trust and attract qualified buyers, the report adds.

So, how exactly should we go about this? The following sections detail your options and how to make best use of them to achieve your goals.

The main post formats

On LinkedIn the key options for publishing are text, video, image and document posts, plus long-form articles. Polls have also been added in 2020.

If publishing on LinkedIn is new to you, it will help to know the basics of how to go about posting before you get into the detail.

- To publish a post or article, go to the Home page (on the top LinkedIn panel) where a box with Start a post can be seen at the top.

- To write a post, click in the Start a post box. This opens the Create a post box into which you type or upload your text.

- To write an article, go to Start a post and click on Write article.

- To add media to a post, click on either the camera, video or document icon, and upload your photo, image, video or document.

- Once the (video/image/document) file has been uploaded, clicking the blue Post button publishes the post immediately. A video takes a few minutes to process before becoming visible.

Begin a post by going to the Home page and clicking Start a post or Write article.

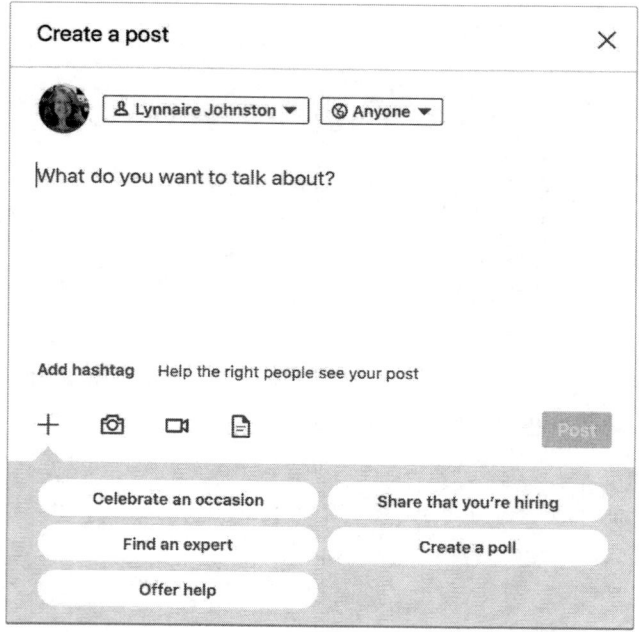

Adding media to your post is as easy as clicking on the image, video or document icon below the text box.

The final step in publishing a post is to click the blue Post button at the bottom right of the post.

Text posts

Text posts (also known as text-only posts) can be up to a LinkedIn-imposed maximum of 1300 characters (including spaces) or around 220 words. They contain no images and text cannot be formatted (bolded, italicised or underlined) from within the platform. The only other elements they can contain are hashtags, @mentions or tags, links and emojis. More on each of these later.

The LinkedIn newsfeed is a busy place so an attention-grabbing headline can be used to entice connections and followers to read your post. This is the case for all types of posts, not just text posts.

When a text post is published in the newsfeed, the first three lines only are visible. To read more, readers must click the See more link. This brings the entire post into view. The aim is to use this introductory section of the post to persuade readers to click See more by making those first three lines stand out.

The problem is that posts display differently depending on the device being used. For instance, one line of text on mobile runs to around 8-10 words, and on desktop 13-15. This makes it tricky to tailor your posts for those first three lines.

I advise writing posts in Microsoft® Word or other word processing programs before uploading to LinkedIn so they can be saved for finishing or uploading later if they are not posted immediately. This provides a permanent record of the post and avoids the danger of losing the text if there is an interruption while writing. Plus, there is no undo button on LinkedIn so if you accidentally delete a block of text, it's gone for good. I suspect those posts which are full of errors were written in a hurry directly into LinkedIn using a phone, instead of being typed first, checked and then uploaded.

Lynnaire Johnston
Word Wizard | NZ's #1 LinkedIn Expert* | Helping you use LinkedIn to achi...
2mo · Edited · ⊕   • • •

Working from home. It'll be the new normal for quite some time!

We have no choice in this so you can either use the time profitably or waste it watching Netflix (appealing, I know!).

Now is the time do all those things you put off because there was always something more urgent, more important (not the same thing!) or more interesting.

Here are a few ideas for what you could be doing with that extra time:

LinkedIn:
☑ Polish your LinkedIn profile – get to grips with the new Featured section
☑ Send out a bunch of personalised connection invites
☑ Ask for recommendations and write them for others
☑ Reach out to LinkedIn connections you've been out of touch with
☑ Prepare content for when things get back to normal

Non LinkedIn activities (from my own to-do list)
☑ Clean out your email inbox
☑ Read all those messages you kept for downtime like this
☑ Complete those courses you signed up for
☑ Go through your website and check for out of date content and broken links
☑ Start/continue/finish that book you have always been going to write
☑ Rekindle relationships and friendships you've let languish
☑ Learn to use that new piece of software you've been putting off
☑ Clean out all the old contacts from your phone

What are you going to do with this enforced downtime?

#creativity

👍 🌐 52 · 39 Comments

An example of a text-only post.

Copying text direct from Word to LinkedIn can cause formatting issues such as additional or missing line spaces (see image next page). The text looks perfect to the writer when it is published but everyone else just sees an inconsistent mess. This is not the professional image you want to portray. If, like me, you are pedantic about these things, the solution is to save your Word document as a Plain text or *.txt file. This strips out any formatting that might cause the post to upload oddly. The text can then be copied from the *.txt file and pasted directly into the post block. Once hashtags, @mentions and emojis are popped in, the post can be published without problems. It might take a little longer but the results are worth it. Using scheduling software such as Buffer can also cause formatting issues.

Text posts work best when they contain just one topic or idea, rather than a multitude, which can become confusing. More complex ideas lend themselves better to articles, where there is no character limit and it is more appropriate to include links (more on this coming up). One option for a more complex subject is to break the ideas into bullet points. Sentences should be kept short and paragraphs limited to two or three sentences. But each person writes in their own way so try out different styles to see what works best for you.

Formatting text posts

It is not possible to make text in posts bold, underlined or italicised from within the platform. But there is a workaround that is particularly good for headlines and can also be used in the body of the post.

Lynnaire Johnston
Word Wizard | NZ's #1 LinkedIn Expert* | Helping you use LinkedIn to achi...
4mo • Edited • 🌐

Marketing rock star Seth Godin coming our way!

I've just heard that this remarkable man is heading our way in May, visiting Melbourne, Sydney, Auckland and Singapore.

Talk about thrilled! I'm right now organising to attend.

It's Seth's first Oceania tour and I understand significant arm-twisting was needed to get him to agree.

I've had several of his books for years – Poke the Box, Meatball Sundae and my favourite, Purple Cow. I'll be rereading them before his half-day event in Auckland on May 20.

I've realised, too, my library of business books is missing his latest, This is Marketing: Making & Sharing Work that Matters. Sounds super relevant to today's world (as all of Seth's material tends to be, if not ground-breaking) so Book Depository will be sending me that.

My library seems to be a fan, as well, as it has several books of his I've not read (now on order) and an audio book he narrates himself, Tribes, which is fascinating.

I don't usually wax so enthusiastic about events, but I'm over the moon about this one! So much so, I might even share some nuggets of his wisdom as I rediscover them.

And if you're keen to go see #SethGodin yourself: https://bit.ly/2U6V4x1

#creativity #marketing #AdvertisingandMarketing

An example of a badly formatted post with unwanted line breaks appearing between sentences.

To format text for LinkedIn posts, do the formatting *off LinkedIn*, copy it and place it back into the post. The website Unicode Text Converter (qaz.wtf/u/convert.cgi) formats text into bold, italic and italic bold among others, in different typefaces. For text that resembles a medieval bible, handwriting or calligraphy there are many fonts to try. Just consider readers who may find fancy script on a small screen difficult to read.

Using this free text converter is easy. Just paste the text you want to format into the bar at the top of the site's page and copy and paste whichever result you prefer from the list below.

This technique can have drawbacks – most notably display. It sometimes adds in unwanted spacings, generally at the beginning of the newly formatted text. Use it with caution.

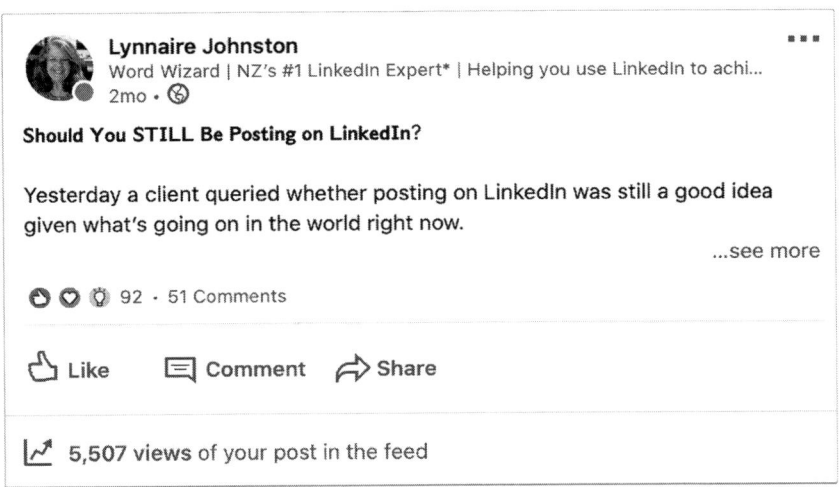

This example of a text post formatted with Unicode Text Converter shows how a headline in bold can stand out from the surrounding text.

Image posts

Most posts in the newsfeed include an image. Sometimes this is the result of a link but equally it could be what is known as an **image post**. In some cases, this will be an image with no text apart from a few hashtags, such as a quote, for example.

Other image posts might be 1300 characters of text with an image added to illustrate the point being made.

Image posts generally perform the least well on LinkedIn in terms of viewership but can be attention-grabbing and showstopping. Often the low engagement numbers are because the post is poorly done. This could be because it is a promotion, for example, instead of providing true value or inviting discussion, which is where LinkedIn's strength lies.

There are plenty of options for using images on posts – but the two styles are: with text and without text. If the image has no accompanying text, the words may need to be superimposed on the image so the meaning is clear. This style is ideal for event promotion and quotes, as in the example on the next page. If the image has no text there is a risk the message will be lost or misunderstood, so accompanying text is needed to explain the details. The inclusion of keywords and hashtags is also essential if the post is to be picked up and promoted by search engines and the LinkedIn algorithm. (See more on the effectiveness of hashtags on page 76.)

LinkedIn is not Facebook, so images are expected to be relevant to the post content and, if they are not, they run the risk of seeming gratuitous and attention-seeking. So, unless your business is photography or something similar, gorgeous photos of sunsets are, I believe, inappropriate. But want to show off a new kitchen you have built for a client? By all means publish a photo but include a mini case study that explains the process, the challenges overcome and the results achieved to ensure biggest bang for your post buck.

It is still true that a picture is worth a thousand words, so each image must count and enhance your message, not detract from it.

Yes, Facebook-style images can attract a lot of views but what does it say about you and your brand or business if you use click-bait instead of providing value? I recommend steering away from self-serving, look-at-me images such as you standing in front of an audience or a selfie with someone famous because part of your audience will just see it as showing off. You could however have the best of both worlds by talking about what you learned from the event or the meeting. Write as if you'd been asked to provide a report for your company on what took place and how it could benefit the organisation.

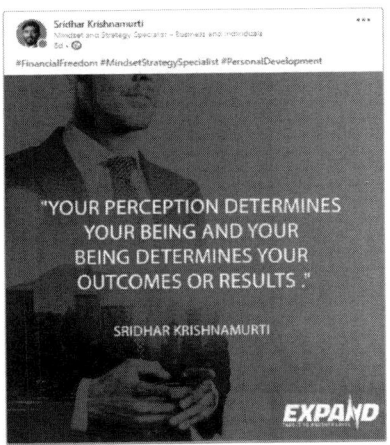

An example of an image post with no additional text except hashtags.

To display well on the LinkedIn feed, your image should be sized correctly. Currently, the optimum dimensions are 1200 × 628 pixels on mobile and 1200 × 1200 on desktop.

When placing text over an image use a sans-serif font (one that does not have extending features or *serifs* at the end of strokes) to make it easy to read on a screen. Steer away from reverse text – light text on a dark background – which is also hard to read. Remember that many people will see your image on a smart phone screen so it will be tiny.

Image posts make a great contrast to other forms of posts though, offering variety to your connections and followers. And as they stand out in the newsfeed make them a part of your posting mix.

Video posts

Video posts are an increasingly popular type of post. They are a great way for connections and followers to see you, hear you and get to know you better. Many videos are quite informal, shot by people at their desks, in the garden, in their cars and even, sometimes on holiday. Videos of events are popular, as are award ceremonies – there is really no limit.

Video uploaded direct from a computer or phone rather than third party apps like YouTube is known as **native video**. This format makes publishing videos very easy and it has been enthusiastically adopted by many.

The basics of video posts

The usual length for a LinkedIn video is one to three minutes as attention spans are limited. However, much longer videos are also common, although I suspect fewer people watch to the end. Those that are unusual or fascinating in some way attract the most views. Posts that go viral, receiving hundreds of thousands of views and reactions, are often video posts.

Many of the videos that pop up in the newsfeed are amateur presentations recorded on a mobile device. The difference in quality between these and a professional production can be massive. Amateur efforts often result in poor light or sound quality, and uneven delivery of the script such as verbalised pauses (um, ah), incomplete sentences and muffled speech.

Video best practice requires that they have captions, simply because many people are unable to *listen* to a video but are able to *watch*, such as in office situations or on public transport. Rev.com is commonly used to provide captions for videos.

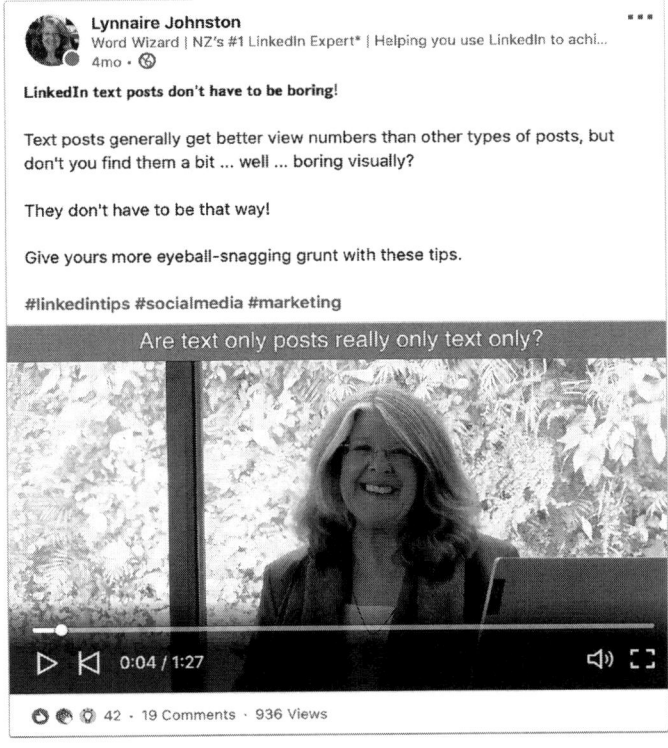

An example of how LinkedIn displays native video with captions in posts.

The quality of videos on LinkedIn ranges from decidedly average to excellent. What makes a video excellent is high quality production, correct dimensions and engaging content.

When posting a video, it is best to include a written introduction that is long enough to trigger the See more button. That way, if your gorgeous face isn't enough to make someone want to click Play, the way you introduce it might be.

There are many styles of video posts. One of the most common is talking head – where someone speaks straight to camera. Animations, event segments and corporate videos also appear on the newsfeed.

Another popular style is the slide technique where there is no voiceover, only music. Words are superimposed on interesting backgrounds that explain clearly and succinctly the point the video is making. This is great for simple, single point, learning-style videos.

Talking head and slide videos can be done relatively easily yourself. But big budget videos requiring a professional videographer show up from time to time, too.

LinkedIn Live – potentially a video game changer

A Facebook feature for some time, LinkedIn has only recently begun to offer live video, known as **LinkedIn Live**, direct to your newsfeed. However, as of writing, it was not yet widely available and is being used by only a few. Once we all have it, live video is likely to go through a stage of being very popular, a phase all new features on LinkedIn seem to go through. It will be great for making announcements, livestreaming events, conducting interviews and running tutorials or classes.

The downsides are plentiful, however. For instance, the sound, lighting, background and other factors all need to be correct which, as anyone who has ever done a video knows, is not as easy as it sounds. If you make a mistake, there's no re-recording; the video has already been broadcast.

Plenty of people will want to use this feature when it becomes widely available, though. And some will be great at it. Others, celebrities or influencers, will care less about the quality and more about being an early adopter of this new technology.

Document posts

Document Posts allow Microsoft® Word files, PDFs, slideshows and other types of documents to be added to posts published from both personal profiles and company pages. In the newsfeed they display as a PDF. When clicked by a viewer, the document opens in a new window where it can be viewed and downloaded, if required. Documents posted on LinkedIn can be single or multiple pages but because many people will look at them on handheld devices, text and image size may be an issue.

This style of post has been doing very well because LinkedIn likes to give new features a good push. As they require some effort to produce this is a good reward but not one that may be long-lasting.

Posts have a limited lifespan in the newsfeed so give them longevity by publishing via the newsfeed first. Then add them to the Featured section of your profile or your current job in the Experience section. That way they can be easily found by viewers of your profile and are permanently available.

One way document posts are of use is in building authority. Sometimes a topic is too complex for a simple 1300-character text-only post and deserves more considered treatment. Or, a document might already be formatted for another use but would also be ideal for LinkedIn. In these situations, sharing as a document post is an excellent idea. As an example, a PDF I put together about video posts reached a respectable 18,000+ views in newsfeeds before LinkedIn stopped showing the view numbers.

Keep in mind that while it is difficult to read an A4 size PDF on small screens, viewers may choose to download it for later viewing on a larger screen, so don't discount document posts on this basis. An excellent size for document posts is that provided by slideshow programs such as Microsoft PowerPoint®.

As with image and video posts, text can be added to introduce a document. Write sufficient text to bring up the ...see more button so the viewer knows what the post is about and decides to read further.

An example of how a document post should look. The size of the document affects the way it displays and this slide deck size works perfectly.

Polls

Polls made a welcome return to LinkedIn in 2020, after disappearing in 2014, and provide a simple way to survey LinkedIn members.

Here's what you need to know about setting up a poll:

- Questions can be up to 140 characters long.

- There can be between two and four optional answers each up to 30 characters long.

- Polls can be set to run for one day, two days, one week or two weeks.

- Polls can be posted from the Home page of both personal profiles and company pages.

- While the poll is live only the author and those who vote can see the results.

- The number of people who have voted is visible to everyone regardless of whether they vote.

- Authors of polls can see the names of those who have voted and which option they have voted for.

- First-degree connections can be messaged from within the poll.

Polls, like all posts, can have accompanying text which is useful for explaining the purpose of the poll, and, perhaps, what you intend to do with the results.

As polls are a bit limited, one good way to use them is to ask a question in the poll, and in the accompanying post ask for additional information via a comment. As comments are noted by the algorithm the post will be distributed to more newsfeeds. Another way to solicit comments is to make the final poll option Other and ask voters to explain in a comment.

On the first poll I published when the feature became available, the ratio of 1st-degree connections to 2nd- and 3rd-degree was close to 50:50. If that ratio is truly representative it makes polls a good source of potential new connections from among those 2nd- and 3rd-degree connections.

LinkedIn promotes polls for canvasing opinions and getting feedback. Respected online news outlet TechCrunch describes polls as 'a quick-fire and low-bar way of asking a question and encouraging engagement'.

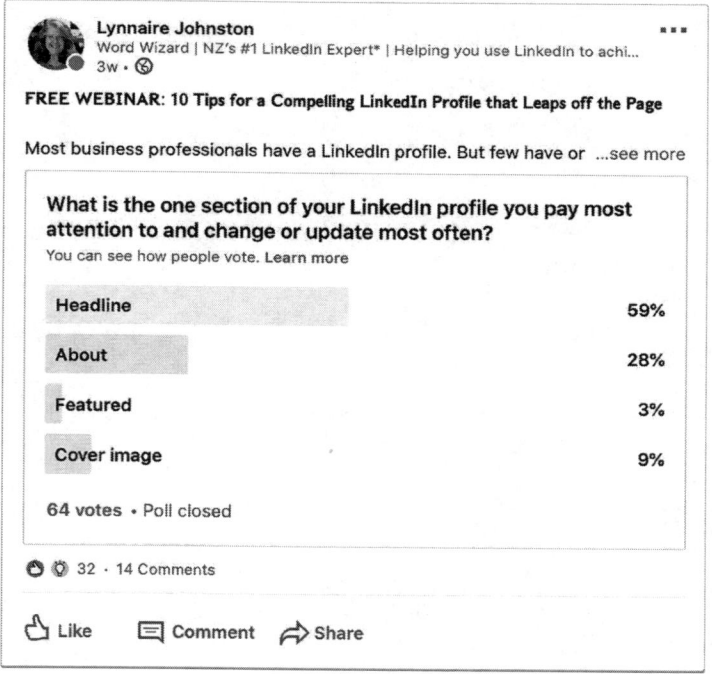

The first poll I posted. The number of votes is at the bottom left, with the days left for the poll to run next to it.

Polls are straightforward and easy to put together. Voting is simple and polls give people more of a voice than a simple like or other reaction. And, as voting is anonymous except to the author, there is a greater likelihood of honesty.

As with any LinkedIn feature, polls will be used in different ways to achieve the publisher's desired results. But I think it likely they will be hugely popular with early adopters for a time and then become a routine alternative to text, image, video and document posts.

Link posts

Although not a formally recognised format, link posts have become common in the newsfeed. A link post consists solely of a link to an external web page which displays the preview of the page. Sometimes there are hashtags but rarely is there any headline or explanatory text – just the link image with a caption beneath. This usually turns out to be the headline on the page the post directs to. Often the link text itself isn't displayed, only the link preview image, and there is nothing indicating you need to click on the image to go to the post.

Posts like this do not lend themselves to engagement or being read, unless the headline is particularly intriguing as there is often little clue as to the post's topic. In order to read the post, people must leave LinkedIn and if they want to engage, they must return to LinkedIn. This has a negative impact on engagement.

It is a lazy way to post that makes no attempt at engagement or sharing value of any kind. My theory is that they are generally uploaded by those who need to fulfil a social media quota and who decide to take the easy way out by dumping in the link. It is the antithesis of the philosophy of giving value, sharing useful material or engaging with others to build relationships but is nonetheless practised widely.

I would argue that valuable newsfeed space is being wasted, too, because without any accompanying text there is no context, explanation or reason to click on the link. Even if a viewer does leave the newsfeed for the article, the likelihood of their returning to your post to engage with it is low.

An example of a link-only post. There is no indication where the link goes or the subject matter. Often the only clue is any potential image that displays. There is no incentive for anyone to click off LinkedIn to go to it.

Using all the available post types

The five styles of posts available – text, image, video, document and polls – allow for plenty of variety. We may prefer one particular type because they are easy for us to produce consistently (text posts are my preferred milieu, for instance), rather than interspersing them with others. The danger of using one style only is that they must be exceptionally engaging and have interesting content in order to persuade LinkedIn members to watch or read every one. ESPECIALLY, if a new post is uploaded every day.

One potential combination is a video post, text post, image post, document post and poll per week. Take care not to overdo it, however, because publishing too many posts is counterproductive as the algorithm will simply ignore them. It is better to have fewer posts of higher quality than to inundate the newsfeed with irrelevant rubbish that adds no value.

Long-form articles

In LinkedIn's early days, it had a section called Pulse, the forerunner of today's articles. Material published in Pulse was hugely popular with both writers and readers as the LinkedIn algorithm ensured it was shared widely. Today, it is vastly different. Now renamed **Articles** and lacking the overt backing of the algorithm, articles are much less favoured than the other forms of posts LinkedIn has now introduced.

The major disadvantage of articles is that they receive far fewer views except in exceptional circumstances. However, they also have much to recommend them, including building credibility.

Articles can be any length but are most often used for publishing long-form content. They can contain images, videos, links and slide shows. The text can be formatted (bolded, underlined, italicised) from within the platform which isn't possible in posts.

Experts have varying views about the efficacy of articles but I believe that because they build up into a library showcasing your knowledge and expertise, they should be included in LinkedIn marketing.

Articles take several hours at least to prepare but are indexed by Google so show up in searches. If writing is part of your professional repertoire, I recommend including them. If you are not a proficient writer and creating 1000-word articles is your idea of torture, don't put yourself through the agony. There are better uses of your time on LinkedIn. The rest of us should continue producing articles several times a year at least.

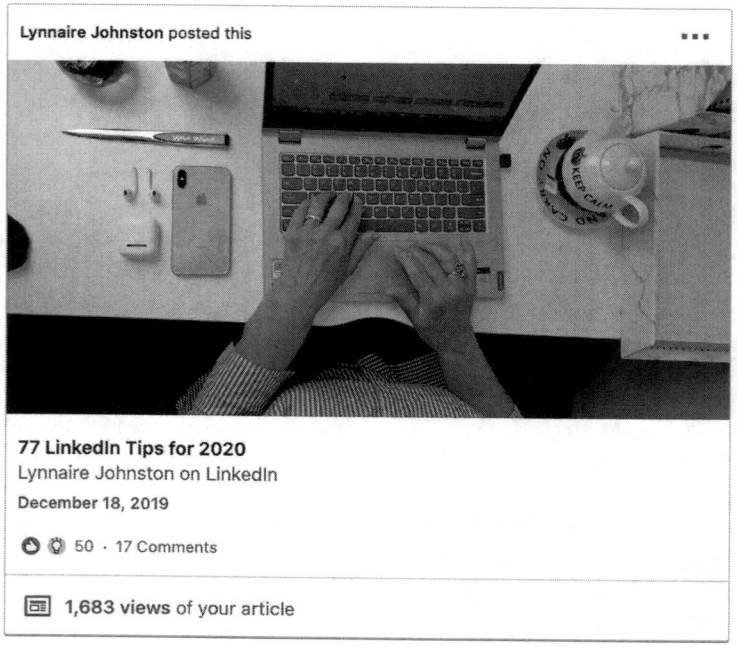

Lynnaire Johnston posted this   **...**

77 LinkedIn Tips for 2020
Lynnaire Johnston on LinkedIn
December 18, 2019

50 · 17 Comments

1,683 **views** of your article

Articles are housed in the Activity section of LinkedIn profiles and display like this.

Articles lend themselves to topics that are more complex than can be explained in a 1300-character (220 words approx.) post. For instance, articles are ideal where:

- There needs to be a balanced viewpoint of both sides of an argument.

- A great deal of information needs to be included to do justice to the topic.

- There is a long list of points to be itemised.

- When visuals or video are needed to clarify the message.

Why publish articles on LinkedIn

Because of their longevity, it is essential that articles be professional and reputation-enhancing. They need to be well thought through, have a logical structure and be competently written with plenty of images, links and subheadings. Here are the seven major considerations for articles, and why they are useful in LinkedIn publishing.

1. Articles are longer than posts – generally by a considerable margin. *The Ultimate Guide to Social Media Post Lengths in 2020* by socialreport.com suggests that keeping articles to 120,000 characters (20,000 words) fits LinkedIn's parameters. That makes it a very lengthy article so if your material is that long, post it as a document rather than an article and add a nice cover to do the piece full justice. Or, break it into smaller pieces that can be published sequentially.

2. Articles allow a catchy bio to be included at the end of the piece. This explains who you are and what you do. This is an opportunity to add a call to action, contact details and a link to your website. You might even want to add a photograph of yourself.

3. Articles can be divided into sections with attention- and search engine-grabbing subheads in large, bold text. Do this well and readers may understand the gist of your article without having to read the entire text. Another alternative is teaser-style subheads designed to catch the eye and break blocks of text into more manageable pieces.

4. Images are encouraged in articles and provide visual appeal. Pictures can carry captions, too, so use them to amplify your message. Images are excellent for showcasing a project, say landscape design, where the aim is to explain the process and show the results. Where there is nothing physical to show and the text is more concept focused, Google delivers up plenty of image ideas to include, although always be careful to observe copyright.

5. More a warning than a suggestion – the longer the text, the more opportunity for errors. Even professional writers have their text checked for mistakes because the eye has a nasty habit of seeing what it wants to see and not what is actually written. It is easy for errors to get past us so we need a third party, a neutral person to check that we have not embarrassed ourselves, because mistakes reflect poorly on us. Posts and articles riddled with mistakes do not make the writer look professional or competent. Rather, the reverse.

6. Using bullet points breaks an article into bite-sized pieces and aids understanding of the text. They provide a way to show what's coming up and divide longer articles into easily digestible chunks. Any emoji that is relevant can be used for this.

7. Articles need a solid structure if the reader is to get to the end without becoming bored and giving up. There are a number of ways to organise material. These include:

    • Chronological – past, present and future.
    • Problem/solution – detailing the problem and then offering a solution.
    • Logical – one point leads to another then to another in sequence.
    • Climactic – surprising the reader with a climax or big reveal at the end.

How to format articles

Whatever you decide works best, it will need a beginning, a middle and an end. The beginning will likely be an attention-grabbing headline. The middle is for the detail of the main points and their supporting ideas. The end could be one or more of a summary, a call to action or a question that invites engagement from connections and followers. I don't particularly favour a question ending such as, 'Who else is using this technique and how is it working?' because it reflects poorly if there is little or no engagement on your article. However, calls to action are a great idea, especially if there is a clickable link that takes the reader to a landing or other website page.

Before beginning to write an article, organise your thoughts and ideas. There are several ways to do this, and one of the best is to:

1. Decide on a topic or a theme that is congruent with your area of expertise and will be of interest to your audience of connections and followers.

2. Write a list of the points to be covered and put them into a logical order.

3. Make a few notes about each one or decide on the key message for each.

4. Know where and how the article will end to ensure it doesn't do so in the middle of nowhere. In other words, conclude with a conclusion.

As they require a great deal more work than posts and I am a great believer in repurposing content, I reuse articles. I do that by structuring them so they can be easily divided into 200-word sections and published as stand-alone posts. I upload the entire article to my website first. Then I publish the individual posts from it over a period of several weeks while Google busily indexes the full piece on my website. Once all the posts are used, I republish the article on LinkedIn with a new heading and intro so that to Google, it looks to be another article on the same topic.

While articles are integral to a complete LinkedIn publishing strategy, they take work and time to prepare. If your core competencies do not include writing, either outsource or forget the idea entirely.

Useful article facts

- Articles that are between 1700 and 2100 words get the most shares on LinkedIn.

- Articles with titles between 40-49 characters perform the best on LinkedIn.

- Articles without video perform better than those with video.

- LinkedIn articles featuring exactly eight images far outperform the rest.

- Google loves LinkedIn so every article you publish is indexed and will show up in Google searches, ahead of other content ranking for the same keywords.

How to zhoosh up posts and articles

As you will recall, the only non-text elements it is possible to include in text posts are hashtags, @mentions, emojis and links. These can be added to any type of post – text, image, video and document – and articles.

Using these devices means greater reach, more visual appeal and a better overall result. Let's look at each of these elements in turn, because they are important to the success or otherwise of your posting.

Adding visual interest with emojis and bullet point lists

The only pictorial elements that can be added to text posts and the sections of posts containing text are emojis. There is a huge range of these tiny icons, use of which will make your posts more interesting and guide the reader's eye to the important points. (There's a great article on how to do this by John Nemo which can be found at bit.ly/2SZP3Sw.)

In some instances, emojis don't display as intended. To avoid difficulties caused by this use emojis only where their intent is obvious (like bulleted lists) so readers will still understand your meaning.

Some people place emojis in their profile headline which gives it colour, breaks up the text and makes the headline stand out. The same warning above about how they display applies though so keep it simple when deciding to use them.

Bullet points are a great way to break up the text of a post or article to make it less dense and easier to read. They are also one of the few methods by which a visual element can be added to posts. There are plenty of relevant choices from different colour and size dots, to pins and ticks including – ◆, ✓, 📍, ●, !, ☞, 🖌, ▶ and more.

Pointing fingers are also a useful addition because instead of being at the beginning of a line, which is where they are most commonly placed, there could for instance be an entire line of downward pointing fingers to highlight the text below. On one client's profile I was updating, I began each line of her list of awards with the trophy emoji (🏆) and the microphone emoji (🎤) for her list of TV, radio and podcast appearances. It looks very effective and stands out. Another connection who has mastered the art of the emoji often uses a single emoji at the end of her sentences and downward facing arrows to indicate the comments box below. This, too, is very effective.

Holly Locastro · 1st
Unlocking B2B Marketing Potential 📝 | Founder | Entrepreneur | Coffee L...
1yr · Edited · 🚫

I'm a lover of technology 😄

But only when it serves a (really) good purpose.

💡 I have no idea how I ever managed my business life without Xero, Monday.com and Active Campaign 💡

They're all the perfect blend of features, support, beautiful interfaces and efficiency.

However, I'm the first to admit, that with other platforms, I get tied too much to the time I've invested in them to change (even if they're not doing what I want) ↓ ↓ ↓

1. There's the time spent researching in the first place.

2. Then assessing and trying it myself.

3. Getting feedback from my team using it.

4. Then onboarding us all (and sometimes clients too).

I need to sit down just thinking about all that effort 😵

However, I had a bit of a reality check when I watched one of my team using one of our platforms ↓ ↓ ↓

1. The amount of time it took him (at least double what it should have).

2. The frustration he was obviously feeling because it was slow.

3. And in the end, the result wasn't exactly what we wanted either.

It was a classic case of (my favourite phrase) "false economy".

We're all busy.

With lots to do.

But there are some things that just need to be done.

I'd love to hear how you manage new tech tools in your business ↓ ↓ ↓
#marketing #marketingtechstack #peoplewithpurpose

In this post Holly Locastro has used face emojis to convey emotions, light bulbs to indicate ideas, and down arrows to move viewers through the text. At the end she has used arrows again as a call to action to solicit comments.

Using bullet points effectively requires a list. When choosing a topic or subject, think about ways to incorporate lists specifically for using bullet points.

Bullets work best with short sentences or sentence fragments – such as:

✳ 700 million LinkedIn members

Shorter is better because text in bullets stands out less when it rolls over to a second line and the bullets don't display on consecutive lines. Of course, this is often the case on mobiles where page widths are extremely narrow so, again, the shorter the bullets the better.

Two more points about using bulleted lists:

- How-to and posts containing bulleted lists perform almost twice as well as question posts on LinkedIn.

- Posts split into five, seven or nine points perform better than block text posts.

The ways bullets can be used to make posts more attractive and easier to read are not limitless but are certainly extensive. Try a few different ways and see what works for you.

Attracting attention through @mentions (aka tagging)

A common technique in posts is to @mention or tag another person. When this occurs, their name is displayed in blue as a clickable link and they receive a notification of their inclusion in the post or associated comments (at least they're supposed to – the system is by no means perfect!).

This is most often used when the poster is writing about another person, including them in a list, or identifying them as being at an event as they appear in the accompanying photo. These are all very valid reasons for @mentioning someone.

LinkedIn in Action

A mid-sized architectural company had an ad hoc relationship with LinkedIn. Every now and again it would post updates about the company and its team members which always got great reach but were quickly forgotten.

The CEO decided to implement a content marketing programme which combined regular posts, engagement and connecting with targeted connections.

Posts became highly successful, often reaching 10,000 views with a high level of organic reaction. This, combined with increasing connection numbers and engagement on others' posts, resulted in the CEO beginning conversations with potential partners, clients and collaborators which led to new opportunities.

• • •

A healthcare consultant wanted to increase his visibility on LinkedIn as a means of finding corporate work. But he was very busy consulting with clients and had little time to spend on producing content.

The solution was to take some of his in-depth work – a keynote presentation and an online webinar – and split these into shorter segments that would be ideal for LinkedIn posts. He ran these as a series of posts and articles that built up a credibility-enhancing library on the platform and which could be displayed on his profile.

This raised his visibility and gave him wide organic reach resulting in increased demand for his services and opportunities to speak at events.

• • •

A budding professional speaker's LinkedIn posts were racking up more views than he had connections – sometimes a lot more. He also had a ridiculously high number of connection invite acceptances; hardly anyone ignored his requests. His secret? Storytelling. A post about his son's toy monkey needing to go to hospital gained thousands of views, proving that well-written content grabs eyeballs. His knack for using stories to convey a

> business message made his story-style posts perfect for LinkedIn. He repeated this feat with further posts about the toy monkey, always relating them back to his primary business message.

The @mention feature allows you to type the @ symbol followed immediately (no spaces) by the person's name (no spaces between the names either). If they are on LinkedIn their name should pop up. Clicking it will add them to your post, the letters turning blue when the post goes live. When commenting on a post the poster's name will come up first in the dropdown list that LinkedIn displays in this circumstance.

Some people abuse the @mention feature quite spectacularly by including a long list of names simply for the purpose of persuading/ bullying/encouraging (take your pick) the people who have been @mentioned to engage with the post. This is considered undesirable LinkedIn behaviour. But honest, careful use of @mentions is seen as an aspect of the sharing, giving side of the platform. Just use the feature judiciously.

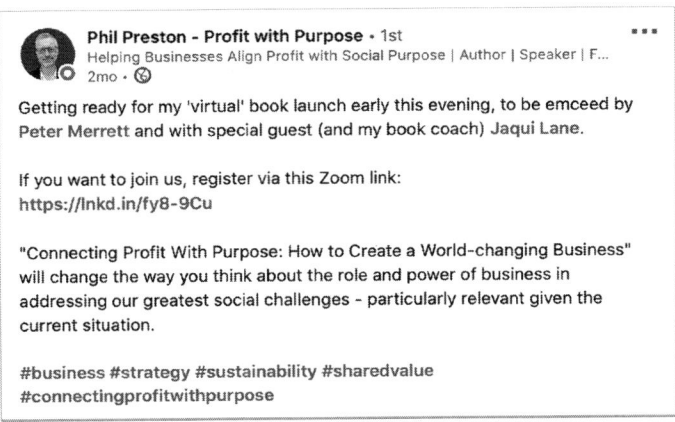

This post includes two @mentions or tags of people – Peter Merrett and Jaqui Lane – whose names display in bolded blue in the live post.

Don't forget hashtags

Hashtags are now as ubiquitous on LinkedIn as Twitter. This is not surprising because they are very useful. You will find hashtags in posts, articles, comments and just about everywhere else on the platform. Most generally, when it comes to posts, they are listed at the end so as not to interfere with the text but some enterprising people use them as word replacements in their posts. While this livens up posts visually it reduces readability and their usefulness in terms of additional views is also debatable. Overuse of hashtags at the bottom of a post looks messy and reduces the number of text characters available.

My view is that it is best not to go overboard. Use them judiciously so they do not become a barrier to understanding.

It had been thought that the more hashtags there were included in a post, the better. But that has been shown to be untrue and the accepted number is currently three. LinkedIn now adds the hashtags used in a post to its URL of the post so choose the most popular for best reach.

Some hashtags have millions of followers but their popularity seems to wax and wane. You can find the number of followers a hashtag has by doing a search for it in the main search box.

I recommend using hashtags on every post you upload, no matter the format used. This will help the post be more visible and seen by a larger number of LinkedIn members.

Hashtags help people searching for content to find your post. If you want your material to be searched for and seen it makes sense to include the more popular hashtags in your posts, provided they are relevant.

Nash Billimoria · 1st
Founder | Consultant | Certified OKRs Coach | Professor. Building purpos...
3mo · 🌐

Why is creating #safety in your #execteam a foundation for fast growth in #tech?

#Leaders of tech companies sometimes assume that their product and their technology are what makes their business thrive.

In the process, they forget that business is a #humansystem.

What we have to understand is that the human brain is a magnificent tool designed for SURVIVAL.

NOT for high performance in the work place.

This means we have to overcome our natural tendency towards fear and self protection.

To build an environment where everyone is #safe to be fully themselves, speak their mind with no fear of ridicule and no need to be defensive.

When this happens, teams get to the root of issues - and then they make those issues go away forever.

This leads to product breakthroughs, capital raising, exponential sales growth and everything else that drives business results.

Without a conscious effort to create safety, teams tend towards dysfunction and poor results.

Quote from Brene Brown:

"Leaders must either invest a reasonable amount of time attending to fears and feelings, or squander an unreasonable amount of time trying to manage ineffective and unproductive behaviour"

- you choose.

#highperformanceteam #scalingup #CEOs #HighImpactCulture

In posts, words written as hashtags are displayed in bold blue type. While they stand out, the brain needs a little longer than normal to translate the meaning of the hashtag symbol, potentially slowing understanding. Judicious use of hashtags has been made of hashtags in this post, but when a post is full of them it can look messy and contrived.

Other issues affecting formatting can be caused by the use of third-party scheduling apps. It is relatively easy to spot scheduled posts in the newsfeed as the text is likely to be all one dense block. There may be no line spaces between the text and the hashtags, either. Emojis and attractively presented bullet lists are also likely to be missing. All in all, it can be one long mess that is both hard to read and visually unappealing.

It is easy to understand the appeal of a scheduler, however. Just set and forget. But it might be more effective to have a human do this, such as a VA or assistant. That way, any response to reactions/engagement can be caught quickly.

Scheduling software also makes it tempting to repeat the same content across all social media platforms. This is rather like attempting to get your message across to a two-year old, a teenager, a millennial and an elderly person, delivered to each and every one using exactly the same words, tone of voice and facial expression. Each social media platform represents a different audience, and each person has a different reason for being there. Trying to be all things to all people is a waste of everyone's time. Your audience on LinkedIn wants (for the most part) posts that are business or professionally oriented. Give them what they want and expect or they will think you don't understand the platform, that you are wasting their time with irrelevant material and that you are not the professional you claim to be. You already know that Google doesn't like repeated material, so if you want good search results for your content on LinkedIn, be original. By all means, repurpose posts from elsewhere but give them new headlines, a new layout and a different call to action. Social media is hugely important in business marketing – give it the respect it deserves and get it right.

How to create attention-grabbing, engaging content

Successful posting on LinkedIn (generally measured by engagement levels) is the result of a combination of factors, one of which is content. The quality of content is therefore of paramount importance.

Posts that are different or stand out in some way can do enormously well. It's not the format that makes the difference, it's the content. Sometimes such posts are funny, sometimes sad, uplifting or inspirational. Often the personality of the poster shines through. They show a vulnerability perhaps, a willingness to help or even an acknowledgement of others' efforts. In other words, the post adds value. It has a purpose, maybe it even adds to the sum of human knowledge, or shares information that is useful to a large number of people. The best posts are positive. They give back.

The exception to this is controversial posts. These can do enormously well too, but are not a comfortable place to be and require bravery. People are quick to judge and often won't read the post thoroughly before wading in with their views. And those who disagree will waste no time saying so. A controversial post I once wrote which included an image (so the lowest scoring of the post types) reached 35,000 views and garnered a number of negative comments before I lost my nerve and took it down. The risk to reputation from a controversial post is high.

Writing attention-grabbing headlines

The first and arguably most important element of any type of marketing writing is the headline or, in the case of LinkedIn posts, the top one to three lines. Get it right and the post will gain attention. Get it wrong and people will pass over it without looking at what comes next.

The main job of a headline is to stop people in their tracks and compel them to read more.

In some situations – such as newspaper articles – headlines should tell the main facts of the piece, but that's not always necessary on LinkedIn. Sure, provide a clue as to what the post or article is about – the subject – but that is not always desirable. Instead, consider alternative approaches such as:

- Starting with a question. One that makes the target audience stop and think.

- Making a bold claim or statement that you go on to either refute or support.

- Telling a story.

Whatever is best for your headline or first sentence, make it memorable. The newsfeed is a busy place so you will have to work hard to turn browsers into readers and persuade them to click the ...see more button.

How to structure posts

Before beginning to write a post, organise your thoughts and ideas. There are several ways to do this, and one of the simplest is to:

1. Decide on a topic or a theme.

2. Write a list of the points to be covered.

3. Put them in a logical order.

4. Make a few notes about each one or decide on the key message for each.

Whatever you write must be congruent with what the audience wants or expects to see. For instance, a robotics engineer writing about gardening without drawing a link between the two is hard for an audience to get their heads around.

Deciding on a call to action

How the post, update or article ends will depend on whether it is informational or sales oriented. If informational, the reader isn't required to do anything but absorb the knowledge.

If sales oriented, end with a call to action and ask the reader to do something. Common examples of calls to action include suggestions to visit a website, call now, email a request (for information, a call-back or a quote) or, on LinkedIn, make a comment.

Calls to action are often written in the form of what could be described as a command, based on the idea that by telling someone what to do, they will be more likely to do it. That's why TV commercials often end in a version of 'Call now to avoid disappointment', which also adds the element of scarcity. Other examples of this tactic are 'only x number left or 'be among the first 50 callers to receive...'

In LinkedIn posts, calls to action are common. Some people end their posts with a link to a longer article or blog on their website, although this causes the algorithm to repress views, as discussed earlier. Others pose a question like, 'How do you use this in your work?' to seek engagement on their post. And still others end with an offer. As in, 'Type YES in the comments below and we'll send you ...'

Use a mix of calls to action or end with a summary or conclusion statement instead. Be sure not to use the same ending every time as you don't wish to be seen to be selling. You're sharing information.

The downsides of promotional posts

Publishing overtly promotional posts on LinkedIn is not the best use of the platform. While you are here to demonstrate your expertise and skill, out-and-out promotion is hard to achieve without looking like a self-centred show-off. This can lose you connections, followers and engagement quicker than just about any other LinkedIn 'sin'.

However, when posting valuable content and regularly sharing information that people want to know, one promotional post a month is perfectly acceptable. It is unlikely people will see it without having first looked at your useful content and so will be more receptive to a promotional-style post.

When writing this type of post it should be couched in terms of the benefits to others. Instead of making it about yourself, make it about how you can help and can solve those problems that keep your readers awake at night.

Many people use photos of themselves on stage or meeting someone important to illustrate their promotional post but some people will not view such posts positively. Instead, find something valuable to share or explain the results you have helped the organisation achieve.

The outcome you want is for people to look at the post and think, 'This is exactly my problem. It looks like they might be able to help. I'm going to get in touch/visit their website.'

The one type of promotional post that does fit with my ethos of sharing and giving is the 'pay it forward' type post. There is no expectation of reward and shows a giving personality.

Example of 'pay it forward' posting

My connection Cedrick Dockery regularly posts about people in his network who are doing great work. He writes about what they do that's different and how they have helped him. Cedrick's posts don't attract a higher number of views than normal so that's not the rationale behind his actions. He simply wants to draw attention to what he sees as good work being done by others. This is something we could all do more of. Imagine if we all wrote a post a month praising someone, without expecting anything in return. There's even a hashtag associated with this, #goingaboveandbeyond, that has nearly 18,000 followers.

Another connection, Mike Restivo, whom I do not know personally and with whom I have no common business interests, regularly shares my material, mentions me in a comment or in some other way promotes my skills. Despite there being nothing materially in it for Mike, he does this consistently. By doing so he shows he's a good person, he stays top of mind with me for potential future business or referral opportunities, and he demonstrates he's connected with other like-minded individuals who share useful material. In short, he is establishing trust and credibility with his audience. Who wouldn't want to do business with someone like Mike?

Choosing the right style

Choosing a style for your posts is something to consider before starting to write. You could, for instance, be:

- Formal or informal

- Super-professional

- Funny

- Serious

- A storyteller.

What about clickbait? This tabloid newspaper method of attracting attention uses outrageous headlines and sometimes gratuitous images which often bear no relation to the text. My advice on overt use of clickbait is… don't. Not on LinkedIn anyway. It may be appropriate on other sites but not on a professional business networking platform where your reputation is hard won and easily lost.

When choosing a style, write in the way that feels most comfortable. And remember, styles can be varied. Try out new ideas and ways of writing. This will expand your skill set and versatility.

One other style element to consider is whether to use big blocks of text or, at the opposite extreme, one sentence per line. Generally I advocate two sentences per paragraph, as in most writing. Three at a pinch.

Deciding what to write about

Many competent and knowledgeable people are put off writing posts on LinkedIn because they don't know what to write about. Here's my advice: write about what you know even if other people might already know the same information. They are unlikely to be sharing it on LinkedIn. This will showcase your abilities as you build a LinkedIn presence.

Practise posting to learn what works best. The more posts you publish, the better you will become at gauging what your audience wants to read or hear about.

If starting a post is a struggle, once you've decided on a topic, go back to my section titled 'How to structure posts' and begin there.

If you have no notion what to write about, here are a few suggestions to spark ideas:

- Do a Google search of your main area of expertise and see what pops up on different news sites. Find something you feel qualified to venture an opinion on and write about the news article from that viewpoint.

- Look on the LinkedIn newsfeed for other posts or articles about your topic (use hashtags to search) and see what others are writing. Often a post by someone else will spark an idea.

- Any time an idea for a post pops into your head – make a note of it. Either write it down or record a voice memo on your phone. If you don't do this the idea may be forgotten by the time you sit down to draft the post.

- What has happened in your business life recently that is worthy of a post? Tip: if it is based on a client, change the details sufficiently so they are not identifiable to themselves or by others.

- Think about personal stories that might have a business message. Especially ones from which you have learned a valuable lesson.

Content ideas truly are limitless. Harness them by spending time thinking about what you know and then marry that with what your clients want to know.

Mistakes to avoid

Once you have written your post, check it for mistakes. Because the eye sees what it expects to see, finding mistakes can be tricky. Also, we tend to dash posts off very quickly without too much thought or attention. This can have consequences. A post I wrote mentioned lack of shipping on the Port Chalmers harbour, Dunedin, at the start of the coronavirus lockdown. What I hadn't considered was someone inferring from my words that the port itself was closed. This wasn't true. To rectify this, I went back to the post and edited it to be crystal clear that I was talking about the inner harbour only. Be careful what you write!

Some people write directly into the publishing box when posting on LinkedIn. I strongly advise against this for several reasons.

1. There will be no permanent record of the post in your files, which can lead to repetition of content.

2. You will be tempted to publish it immediately on finishing, which means it won't sit with you and percolate. I'm a strong believer in separating writing from publishing because returning to a piece after an interval almost guarantees there will be something to improve or change. This is truly an important piece of advice if your post is in any way controversial or derogatory.

3. Should there be an interruption while writing, the post won't be automatically saved and could be lost.

4. You are highly likely to have made a spelling or grammatical error, missed out a word, repeated a word, forgotten to add a full stop at the end of a sentence or misplaced an apostrophe. Posts need editing, correcting and proofing – preferably by an expert. Even as a word wizard, I have my own work proofed by a professional copy editor who ensures my errors remain unpublished.

If however professional help is not an option, here's how to reduce the likelihood of errors:

- Print out your text.

- Read it out loud.

The extra time you take to do this step could make the difference between being seen by LinkedIn members as a professional or as an amateur. Your own skill as a writer will determine how much extra effort you will have to make to ensure your text is accurate. Don't spend forever on it, just keep in mind that mistakes reflect badly on us, making us look sloppy and unprofessional.

Building a posting plan that works

One of the main barriers to posting or publishing on LinkedIn is content. Not knowing what to write or post and not being a good or confident writer are the two most common reasons clients give when explaining why they don't post. They understand the benefits of posting and how a programme of regular quality posts will benefit their reputation and career, but they let their perceived inadequacies prevent them from doing so. As this activity is the one that builds visibility on LinkedIn, it is important to know how to do it well and the pitfalls to avoid.

What makes posts stand out is their quality. And quality comes from knowing an audience well, what they want to read. It comes from taking time to construct posts, tailoring posts to the LinkedIn platform (NOT copying the exact same text from Facebook or Instagram), using all the platform's options and above all not being boring!

The best way to publish well on LinkedIn is to have a posting plan. This will bring together the key aspects of a posting programme into one document that acts as a bible. It covers elements such as posting timetable, type of post, topics, sources of information, other uses for the content, delegation and deadlines.

This is a very simple version of a plan that could be used by multiple people who may be contributing in some way. It might also include the posting date and the URL of the post so you will always be able to find it and view the engagement metrics. I would recommend planning at least six months ahead. This allows plenty of time for the preparation of videos and documents that may involve the assistance of others.

One week of it might look like this:

	Objective	Topic/subject	Format type	Content source
Monday	Authority building	Tips on area of expertise	Text	To be written
Tuesday	Creating trust	Personal experience	Image	Own content library
Wednesday	Timeliness	Industry development	Video	Record new series
Thursday	Engagement	Offer a free ebook, white paper, case study	Document	Existing marketing material
Friday	Promoting others	Website host	Text	To be written

Your posting plan might be your content bible but it isn't set in stone so can be changed to reflect new developments and ideas that mirror your business. It shouldn't be created and then consigned to the bottom drawer like that expensive marketing or business plan. Create it once, create it well and use it often.

Here are a few basic content ideas to get started:

- Seasonal events as they relate to your business or industry (e.g. spring or holidays).

- Company events or milestones that can be taken advantage of (new premises or office).

- Industry changes or news.

- Personnel achievements that reflect well on the person and the organisation (a successful fundraiser, sports win or business award).

- General news that has a bearing on your industry such as, if you're in the insurance business, a major earthquake/hurricane/forest fire that could have longer term effects on policyholders.

Content creation is a strange thing. The more you do it, the easier it becomes. Every thought, every activity, every client interaction, every post or article you read, or video you watch may spark an idea for a post. Not all ideas will be good ones, but ideas beget ideas and once you turn your head toward content for posts, you'll be amazed at how many possibilities there are. My secret is to write the idea down as soon as I can, then when I'm stuck, go to my list of post ideas and choose one that inspires me.

Depending on your areas of skill, one or two types of posts are more likely to appeal to you than others. Go with the flow on that while working to improve your other areas. For me, as a writer, text posts are the fastest and easiest, the biggest bang for my buck. Image posts traditionally don't do well for me so I post fewer of them. And videos present a huge technical barrier. It could be the same for you with, say, text posts or articles – you're just not comfortable writing. Given that's a basic skill that we all need to master in order to progress in our careers or businesses, I suggest you work to overcome that. Whether that's taking a writing class, practising like crazy or out-sourcing to a professional writer – don't let your lack of prowess in the writing department hold you back.

Barriers to LinkedIn posting plans

Developing a posting plan can take some time but the best way to overcome this is not to go it alone. Bring together a range of people from the organisation – including production/operation team members or those at the coalface – and brainstorm ideas. Write down everything the participants come up with, no matter how oddball. Give these to your content creator (who can be in-house or external) to develop the ideas and draft up copy.

Text and image posts are the easiest to produce, video and documents will take some longer-term planning to put together. However, with the huge amount of content online now in video format, we should all be thinking about ways to produce quality video content that doesn't cost the earth. But make no mistake, company videos need to be professional. A selfie-video might cut it for smaller organisations, but not for those wanting to present themselves as credible, industry-leading and professional.

Because of the complexity of setting up and administering a posting plan, to say nothing of the writing required, many organisations who recognise the advantages of LinkedIn posting outsource the management of their LinkedIn. It saves them time and money, and generally they end up with a better quality of LinkedIn posts.

When it comes to posting, my first instinct is to share. I don't hold back information that would be of value to others. My personal philosophy in life, including LinkedIn, is to help where I can. When someone asks me a question, usually via LinkedIn direct message, I don't hesitate to answer it if it's within my expertise to do so. Where it isn't, I refer them to someone or some information that *can* help.

The LinkedIn community generally – or at least the parts of it I'm involved with, mostly business professionals – is a giving one. Take a look through the newsfeed and you'll find plenty of people sharing information of use to others. It's one of the great things about the platform, in my opinion.

Important posting tips

When to post

As one of the objectives of posting is to increase visibility, people are often concerned with when to post to achieve best results. While opinions differ, the general consensus is that posts will get more viewers if they are uploaded during business hours Monday to Friday, with the most popular days being Tuesday, Wednesday and Thursday. Some people suggest that the best times of day are early morning and late afternoon (before 9am and 4–6pm). If this matters sufficiently to you, try different times on different days and see what results you get (you will need to keep other variables like format, hashtags and so on the same for accurate results).

Frequency of posting

Frequency of posting is another hotly debated topic. If posting daily Monday to Friday is possible, that would be my recommendation but not at the expense of quality content. One post per week is insufficient to get you noticed and two should be the minimum. If posting on company pages, LinkedIn recommends doing so daily to build a following. Conversely, there is evidence that posting more than twice a day causes the algorithm to repress the second post and ignore the third. But try it and see. What you are aiming for is consistency over the long term. LinkedIn publishing isn't a short-term strategy, it needs a commitment of 12 months to be fully effective.

Engagement

More important than either of these is engagement. **Posts of any kind will perform much better if they receive reactions (likes, comments, shares).** That's because reactions lead the algorithm to believe the content of your post is good quality, so it pushes the post out into more newsfeeds. Without this early engagement your post runs the risk of sinking like a stone.

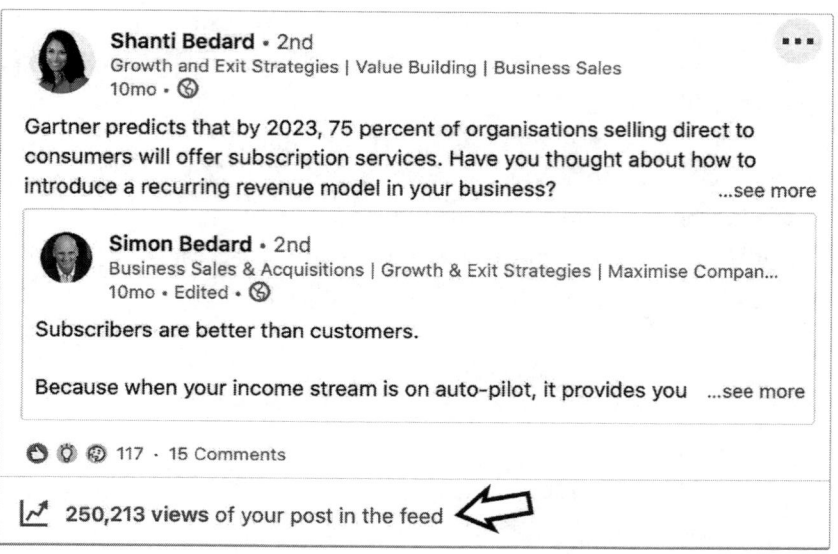

Most shared posts do not perform well in terms of views. This one is an exception, racking up more than 250,000 views. A second shared post by the same LinkedIn member published not long after this one achieved another 220,000. An extraordinary result for which there is no logical explanation.

It can't be any old engagement, either. A handful of likes won't cut it. The post will need comments, the holy grail of reactions. Shares are not particularly useful except on rare occasions when views have been inexplicably known to go ballistic. (See image.) But just because one post goes viral, don't expect LinkedIn to cut you a break next time. It's back to ground zero every time. It doesn't matter what type of like the post receives – the blue hand 'like', the green 'celebrate', red 'love', yellow 'insightful', purple 'curious' or the new mauve 'support' – they all have the same value. Engagement is so important to the success of publishing on this platform that I devote an entire chapter to it in this book, and that chapter is coming up next.

How LinkedIn differs from other social media platforms

One other important point to make about posting on LinkedIn: It is NOT the same as other platforms and needs to be treated differently (and with respect, I would argue). It is ill-advised to simply copy Facebook and Instagram posts and paste them to LinkedIn. There are four principal reasons.

1. Google doesn't like repetition and will likely penalise your post should it spot that you have used it elsewhere.

2. The formats are different and what works on Facebook or Instagram may not work on LinkedIn.

3. The type of material being shared on the platforms is different. Facebook is more about personal and family matters – eating out, holiday photos, cute puppies and so on.

4. The demographic for LinkedIn varies from those of Facebook (people 40+) and Instagram (young people) by covering the entire adult age spectrum.

LinkedIn is a business platform first and foremost.

LinkedIn is a business platform first and foremost. It therefore has a different focus and the content posted should reflect that. Which isn't to say that if you had an amazing business insight while on holiday in Slovenia, you shouldn't share that. By all means explain what prompted the a-ha moment or illustrate it with an image of a local landmark but the backdrop should be an adjunct to the post, not the theme of it. People are in a different frame of mind when they are on Facebook or Instagram – they are looking to relax and take their mind off work. On LinkedIn, people are focused on business and looking for entirely different types of information. Think about LinkedIn as Facebook for business and you won't go wrong.

LinkedIn view counting

LinkedIn does not count views of the different post formats in the same way. So comparing video views with text post views, for example, is like comparing apples and bananas.

Text posts are counted as views when the algorithm places them in members' newsfeeds. It does not even need to be read to be measured, say by the triggering of the ...see more button.

Image posts views are counted the same way. If it's in a newsfeed, it's a view.

Document posts are also counted the same way as text and image posts – by being placed in the newsfeed (known as impressions by geeks). The document itself doesn't have to be opened to be counted as a view.

Videos are the exception to the above and it's a bit complicated so bear with me. They are counted as a view ONLY after the video has been running in someone's feed for at least three seconds. This number is shown on the post where it can be viewed by anyone. However, behind the scenes of video posts more information is available to the poster (see image on the next page). Click on the number of comments below the video and a new screen opens with such useful information as the total number of minutes the video has been viewed (including for less than three seconds), the number of times the video has been watched for more than three seconds and the number of unique viewers. This tells you, for example, that a video with 973 total views might have 933 unique views indicating that 40 people have watched it more than once. There is also a graph that provides further viewing information.

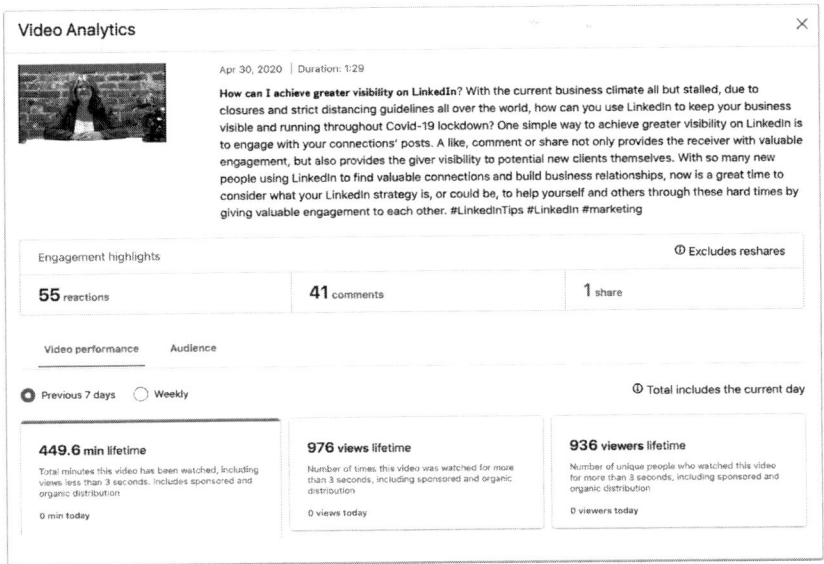

The information available to posters of videos about the performance of their video. This screen also includes the text of the post accompanying the video. To bring up this screen, click on the number of views which is displayed under the video.

For around two weeks after any type of post is published, viewer numbers generally continue to rise, and then plateau. LinkedIn will display the number of views for a few months but dispenses with them eventually. It continues to display like, comment and share numbers, however.

The best tool I've found for tracking LinkedIn post numbers is Shield which is a paid app that can be found at shieldapp.ai. You can see at a glance how posts are performing in any given timeframe.

A much better way than views to determine LinkedIn posting success is to monitor engagement levels – the number of likes, comments and shares that posts receive. And to keep in mind when writing posts or preparing videos, that the aim of this is to share useful information people want to know and encourage engagement with your posts, thereby increasing your visibility in the community.

LinkedIn advertising

As you might know, at the end of 2017 Facebook changed its algorithm so business page posts no longer routinely show up in personal newsfeeds, seriously reducing their reach. People had to move to Facebook advertising to stay in front of their audience.

Fortunately, with LinkedIn, organic reach still rules. At some point LinkedIn may well move to the Facebook model but for now posts on LinkedIn do not require being paid for to reach their intended audience. This is one of the major advantages of LinkedIn publishing.

LinkedIn offers advertising but those I know who have used it report that it is expensive and out of range for most small businesses, although prices reduced during Covid-19. If the product or service being offered has a high price tag or the lifetime value of the client is considerable, advertising could be economic. It is also reportedly not as easy to use as Facebook ads and can be done only from a company page, not a personal profile.

Still, if you decide to go down that route I suggest you dovetail it into your organic posting as well as your other marketing and advertising activities. LinkedIn advertising is a complex and specialist activity that should be part of broader marketing campaigns. I would recommend using an expert for this or you could lose a lot of money for no significant gain.

Top LinkedIn posting tips

1. Text-only posts receive the highest views.

This may be true, and it may not. LinkedIn counts views on text posts differently than video posts so it's hard to know. But they're both popular.

2. Only post videos that have captions.

Many people can't listen to a video if they are in an office, travelling or don't have headphones. Give them the opportunity to see your text instead, via captions.

3. Be professional in your videos.

LinkedIn is a business platform so videos should be about your business or at least business related. If videoing yourself be warm, friendly, personable and professional.

4. Make videos technically proficient.

For the most professional results possible use a lapel mic to improve voice sound and avoid recording in bright sunlight or poorly lit, dark rooms.

5. Document posts display best in the dimensions of a PowerPoint slide presentation.

If creating a document specifically for LinkedIn, do so using the slightly rectangular size of a slide. Documents can be up to 100Mb and 300 pages. Add a title cover.

6. Text-only posts can be made more visually appealing by adding emojis.

This is extremely useful for bulleted lists and can include 🔑, ☞, ✓ and so on.

7. Bold, italicise or underline text.

Load text into qaz.wtf/u/convert.cgi and choose from the options for display. This can affect the formatting or layout of the text once posted but is ideal for headlines.

8. Use three hashtags only at the end of each post.

Overuse of hashtags does not help a post gain more views and reduces the amount of text that can be included.

9. Make hashtags relevant to the post.

Choosing hashtags that have large numbers of followers is an effective way to increase organic reach.

10. Don't tag people in posts in the hope they will comment.

This strategy doesn't work; it only irritates those who have been irrelevantly tagged. Do, however, tag people who appear in photos you post.

11. Articles still have a place in LinkedIn publishing.

While articles are more time-consuming to produce, they are important for topics that require more than 1300 characters. They build into a library that increases your credibility. Aim for at least one article per quarter.

12. Post quality content.

Writing posts that help others by sharing information or providing tips is **the best way to build a following.**

13. All post views are not created equally.

Text, image and document post views are counted differently from video views so cannot be easily compared in terms of effectiveness.

14. Headlines grab eyeballs.

Start each post with a strong headline to entice viewers to trigger the ...see more button

15. Publishing only promotional posts is not best practice.

Upload one promotional post for every nine value-added posts.

16. Check for mistakes.

Check and double-check every post before it is published to ensure there are no errors.

Summary

The ability to publish different types of content is one of LinkedIn's chief points of difference. Especially given that content is most generally based around business. With organic reach still possible (it doesn't have to be paid for like Google AdWords or Facebook Boost), it is a level playing field for anyone who cares to join in. But some techniques are better than others for different reasons and the key is to decide what to do, how often, the type of content to publish and then commit to it.

LinkedIn offers five types of post – text, image, video, document and poll – all of which should be used if publishing regularly. Longer form articles are ideal for content that doesn't fit the constraints of the five post types. Because they remain permanently on a profile articles enhance credibility, making their role a key one.

To enliven the plain appearance of posts use images, emojis, hashtags and @mentions.

Other factors to consider when publishing are style, organisation, content and what the post is expected to achieve.

When considering what content to write about, take into account the resources at your disposal for producing it – it may be faster and more effective for you to write text-only posts, but if you have a large image library you can create material around your images, or if you are a video diva, lean heavily on these assets. Your organisation also might have a large content library that is in document form. All of these – and more – are at your disposal for LinkedIn publishing. Take into account such elements as hashtags, @mentions, emojis, bulleted lists, calls to action and headlines when preparing posts as they all play a part in the success or otherwise of posts.

Posting on LinkedIn is hugely under-utilised yet the audience is made up of LinkedIn members in the top echelons of companies who are decision-makers. Exactly the people you may be wishing to reach! To be noticed by these decision-makers you need to stand out from others who are like you and who offer what you do. In other words – know your audience and deliver the material they want to hear. Do so in a thought-provoking, value-added, consistent manner and your name will be one they look out for in their newsfeeds.

LinkedIn by the numbers

- The LinkedIn feed attracts 9 billion content impressions every week making it an ideal place to share content.

- 40% of active monthly users use LinkedIn daily, increasing your chances of being seen and your content being read and noticed.

- Only three million users share content weekly. That's not much for a very great number of people looking for it – proving that it is massively under-utilised.

- Only 0.59% of posts from B2B marketers come from LinkedIn company pages, but they generate over 10% of leads.

- LinkedIn is the top place to find quality content according to 91% of marketing executives. Other social media platforms were down in the 20s.

- More than half of all social traffic to B2B websites and blogs comes from LinkedIn.

- 92% of B2B marketers include LinkedIn in their digital marketing mix.

- 94% of B2B marketers use LinkedIn for content distribution.

Source foundationinc.co

Checklists

Checklist for posts

Under 1300 characters	
3 relevant hashtags	
Attention-grabbing headline or first line/s of text	
Tagging or @mentions where appropriate	
Text bolded, italicised or underlined where appropriate	
Call to action at end	

Posting Dos and Don'ts

The Right Way to Post	The Wrong Way to Post
Using all 1300 characters available for text posts to fully explain your point.	Making the post too short. Worse, making it only a link and nothing more.
An eye-catching headline that makes people want to read more.	Including too many hashtags (three is considered best practice).
Sharing valuable content so others can learn from you.	Tagging people you want to engage on the post (hint: it rarely works).
An explanation of your image if it's not self-explanatory.	Not explaining in the text there's an external link to an article.
Telling stories that substantiate your message.	Posting like it's Facebook not LinkedIn.

Engaging

The low-key but effective way to be noticed

In this chapter:

CONNECTION BETWEEN people in positive ways is one of LinkedIn's strengths. The most common method of engaging on LinkedIn is through the publishing platform where people interact with each other's posts.

Officially known as engagement, this is when a member uploads a response to a post or article written and published by another member. A post is said to have engagement when it has been liked, commented on or shared in the newsfeed. These are also known as reactions.

'Comments are a great way for members to engage with other professionals on topics that matter the most to them. Friendly discussions and respectful debates are encouraged.' – LinkedIn

The strategy of engaging

Engagement as a strategy entails reaching out to other LinkedIn members for a two-fold purpose – helping them and helping ourselves. Engaging with another person's post (and it doesn't matter if it's a 1st- or 2nd-degree connection) allows them and their work to be seen more widely and for you to be seen more often, too. It's a win-win strategy.

I first saw this as a potential marketing tactic while running a LinkedIn workshop during which one of the attendees mentioned that his main form of marketing on LinkedIn was through comments. He devotes a few hours every week to going through his newsfeed to find posts of interest and relevance to his field and then writes value-added comments on them. This person is very focussed on results and wouldn't be doing it if he wasn't getting them.

One of the advantages of this as a strategy is that it allows you to piggy-back off other people's content. There are several benefits:

- You don't need to create as much content of your own.

- By writing quality, attention-worthy comments you stand out from others.

- If the person who wrote the post has high numbers of followers or the post has generated many views, your chances of being seen and noticed increase.

One of the many appeals of LinkedIn is that it is a level playing field. Anyone can post about any topic and, by extension, anyone can comment on anyone else's posts or articles – whether they are directly connected or not. So, if a post by a 3rd-degree connection appears in your newsfeed you are as entitled to add your two-cents' worth as their first-degree connections.

Types of engagement

There are three types of engagement (also called Reactions) – Likes, Comments and Shares.

A **Like** is the most common form of engagement and shows appreciation for the content and the effort. Likes appear in several versions: a thumbs-up (blue), handclap (green), outstretched hand with heart (support), heart (red), light bulb (yellow) and face (purple). They indicate like, congratulations, support, love, insightful and curious, respectively. They can be used on any type of post or article but someone wanting to like a post can choose only one. The post may end up with likes in several of the styles, as in the screenshot below. The most commonly used like is the blue thumbs-up, but it carries the same weight with the algorithm as all the others.

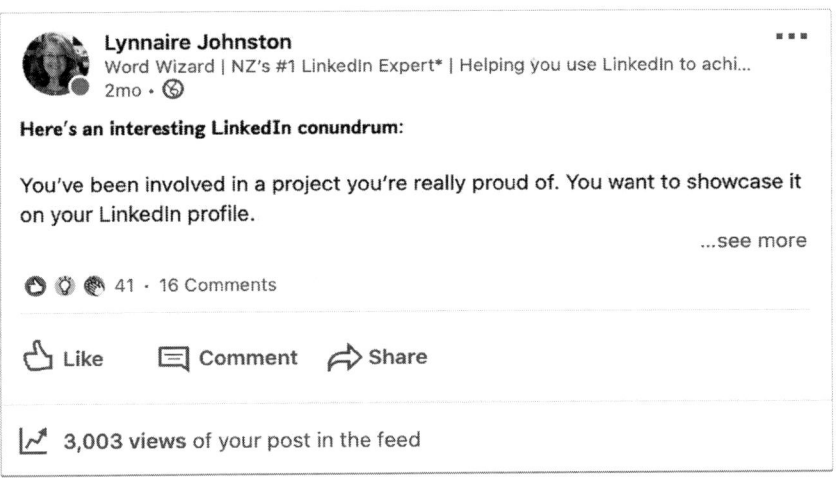

This post has received three different types of likes – the blue thumbs-up, yellow insightful and green congratulations. Clicking the number next to the likes (in this case 41), brings up the list of people who liked the post.

Comments appear in boxes below posts as a thread. To add a comment click on comment below the post which opens the Add a comment box. Anyone may add a comment to any post, irrespective of whether the post has been written by 1st-, 2nd- or 3rd-degree connection.

A **Share** occurs when a new post is created that incorporates a post published by someone else.

To share a post click the share button below the post you want to share.

A share box opens where you can add text and choose who you share it with.

Each form of engagement (like, comment, share) is counted by LinkedIn and is one way the algorithm decides whether or not to place the post in more newsfeeds. As a general rule of thumb, the more engagement there is on a post, the more newsfeeds LinkedIn pushes it out to, resulting in more people seeing it.

Think about your own newsfeed. Do you sometimes find yourself reading a post by someone who is a 2nd-degree connection, which is in your newsfeed because a 1st-degree connection liked or commented on it? The post is unlikely to have shown up without the benefit of that engagement. This is another good reason to have a large network of connections – a wider variety of material appears in your newsfeed.

All engagement is not created equal

Each of the three LinkedIn engagement types (likes, comments, shares) is valued differently by the algorithm. Likes are the least important and comments the most important. Posts with a high number of comments are more widely distributed by the algorithm than those with few or none and thus the post receives higher view numbers.

Shares are the least effective of the three reaction types and posts that are shared usually receive very few likes and comments. However, every now and again a shared post will gain incredibly high views. Take the one on the next page. It generated nearly 33,000 views but received just 31 likes and four comments. There was no logical explanation for this.

Example of a shared post that received an unusually high number of views.

Quality of comments

Comments are displayed by LinkedIn as Most Relevant (the default) or Most Recent. Which of these you want to see can be changed at the bottom of a post, at the top left of the comments. The choice of most relevant means comments that are the most pertinent to the post will be at the top. Those that are viewed by the algorithm as of lesser value will be further down the list. Choosing to display posts by most recent only changes the setting for that particular post.

To be seen by as wide a cross-section of LinkedIn members as possible comments should add value to the discussion, be relevant to the topic and never overtly promotional. Keep in mind that the Activity section of your profile displays your most recent engagement and you do not want it to look like this:

An example of an Activity section with poor quality comments.

A profile visitor spotting this might think that the person does only the bare minimum instead of truly engaging with content. Based on this they might decide whether or not to connect, or conclude the person is half-hearted in their LinkedIn efforts. Compare that with this Activity section:

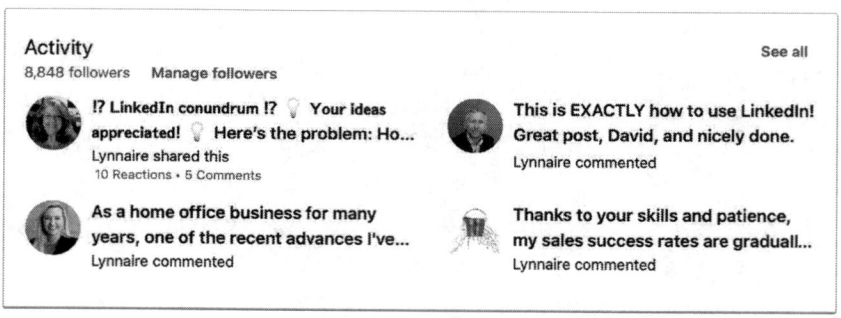

An example of an Activity section with high quality comments.

Comments generally fall into three categories:

- Low value – e.g. 'thanks for sharing', 'great post', 'well done on sharing this'.

- Medium value – go further than a low value comment and might agree with the poster but doesn't add much extra value.

- High value – sharing insights, asking questions, wading into the debate, offering an opinion.

Of these three, the third is the most useful to both parties – the poster and the commenter. The commenter looks good for engaging in the discussion and even better if they add valuable insights that were not included in the original post. There is a great deal of power to be had by demonstrating in a low-key way your grasp of particular subjects that others might not understand or your solutions to problems that others are grappling with. But take care to stay on the subject of the post and not divert it onto a new path. That will not win you any friends and will seem as if you have misunderstood the post's content.

US marketing company Mann & Co suggests six types of comments to leave on posts:

1. **Follow-up questions** – this allows the poster to expand their original content and demonstrate expertise.

2. **Constructive feedback** – pointing out another angle the post could have covered gives the poster the opportunity to write a comment that adds more to the post or create a new post about it.

3. **Answer other commenters' questions** – if the poster doesn't engage with the comments and readers' questions remain unanswered, answer them yourself! Your efforts will be noticed by the questioner if you tag (@mention) them into your answer.

4. **Compliments** – this type of comment is written far too often as seen in the Activity section screenshot on page 110. But when combined with one of the other comment types in this list it will pack a great deal more punch.

5. **Add value** – this can be done by giving an example that reinforces the poster's viewpoint or contributes a relevant link or resource. However, this is not recommended if the poster has already included a link to their own website or blog.

6. **Make a promise** – say you will be sharing the post on other social media platforms or request permission to circulate it among team members.

Keep this list beside you when engaging in comment marketing and you'll never be short of a prompt to spark ideas.

Don't think that just because other people keep their comments short, you need to do the same. Some people write quite long ones. The space allowed is 1250 characters (around 230 words) so write two or three sentence paragraphs for as long as it takes you to say everything. But be careful of writing over-long comments as they can dominate the thread.

Links and images can also be added to comments. But when adding a link in a comment on someone else's post beware of diverting people away from the discussion at hand (which is unforgivably rude) as once they are gone, the odds are they won't return! As well as links, comments can contain emojis (great for lists, see Chapter 2), hashtags and @mentions or tags.

Should you happen to disagree with the content of a post, feel free to say so. You are entitled to your opinion. However, refrain from calling the poster an idiot or attacking them personally. By all means disagree, but disagree with the idea, not the person.

One final tip for quality commenting: tag the person who wrote the initial post or, if you are replying to another commenter, tag them in your comment. This way they will be more likely to see your comment in their notifications and may return to the post to engage further.

If the post is high quality and of interest to others, tag them into your comment (or comment only with an @mention) so they receive a notification. But don't take this to extremes by tagging lots of people. Tag only a few and restrict it to those who would find it the most relevant and useful.

Complimentary comments

Another form of commenting that seems to do well and dovetails with the sharing aspect of LinkedIn is complimenting others. I mentioned this as a post idea in the previous chapter, but compliments work equally well when they are comments.

Take this example of a reaction on a post written by my connection Mike Retivo:

> *'Special appreciation and recommendation to Lynnaire Johnston whose free articles and comments are most valuable to optimize success from LinkedIn participation for business.'*

Now, Mike doesn't just do this form of paying it forward occasionally, he does it regularly. This despite the fact we do not know each other, are on opposite sides of the world in non-aligned industries and unlikely to do business together. This is true LinkedIn citizenship – one person helping another with no expectation of gain. It has significant benefits such as:

- **Building a relationship** – I won't forget Mike's kindness in a hurry.

- **Encouraging reciprocation** – I make sure to comment on his posts where possible.

- **Paying it forward** – good things happen to those who help others without expectation of reward.

- **Demonstrating leadership** – it sets a great example that others might emulate.

This is a particularly good way to use comment marketing in LinkedIn relationship building – but only when it's authentic. Contrived compliments are obvious, thereby doing more harm than good, and potentially implicating the original poster too.

LinkedIn in Action

A landscape gardener in a small city didn't really think that having a presence on LinkedIn would greatly help his business but agreed to have a professional profile created. His connection numbers were comparatively low to begin with but nonetheless he began actively engaging with others' posts as a way of being visible on the platform.

His connection numbers gradually climbed and he became connected with others in his own and associated industries. As his target market – property owners – is also on LinkedIn, it wasn't long before he was approached to provide a quote on a large job, which he ultimately won. He put this down to having a strong LinkedIn profile and considerable visibility in his local market.

• • •

A young marketing manager wanted to move up the career ladder and realised the best way would be to meet and network with higher level managers in her industry. But she lived in a regional city and opportunities for in-person meetings were small. She decided to use LinkedIn to connect with and get to know the people she hoped might become future employers.

After sprucing up her profile, she upgraded to a Premium account and began a targeted campaign of searching for and sending personalised connection invitations to industry leaders and influencers. She carefully followed up acceptances with thank you messages and found ways to stand out by asking how she might help them, engaging on their posts and supporting their LinkedIn activity. Within a year she had been invited to not one but two job interviews, one of which was perfect for her.

How NOT to comment

But where there's good, the bad also lurks. And, in terms of comment marketing, one of the worst sins is to hijack another person's post.

Hijacking occurs when a LinkedIn member writes a comment about their own business that has no relevance to the original post. These types of comments are usually promotional and often don't even make sense. There is no mileage in hijacking another person's post, no matter what the circumstances. It simply isn't in the spirit of LinkedIn and reflects badly on you.

What can you do if your post is hijacked in this manner? Take the comment down quietly and without drawing attention to it. LinkedIn allows you to curate comments so when someone comments negatively or stupidly on a post simply remove it. It is unlikely that a 1st-degree connection is the offender, but if that is the case consider disconnecting from them. You could message them privately and ask them to desist or you will report them to LinkedIn. That might discourage them from targeting others in the same way.

Other forms of negativity can be people disagreeing with your post. See that as a good thing. On a recent post of mine about how to create a long LinkedIn headline, a commenter said he thought long headlines showed someone was trying too hard. At the time, I had a long headline, but as he was entitled to his opinion, I thanked him for the input and left it at that.

Your activity is noted

Depending on the number of likes a post receives, the profile photographs of likers appears at the end of the post, thereby giving them exposure on LinkedIn. As well, the author of a post can view a list of those who have liked the post and again, the liker's image appears. To stand out in these lists, choose a different reaction to the blue thumbs-up.

It is worth noting that some people will notice whether or not you interact with their material. A long-time connection of mine whom I know personally messaged me privately about my lack of interaction with her posts. She said I had never once liked any of them. Regardless of whether she was right – quite likely as I see only a fraction of the posts published in my newsfeed – the point was valid. Further, I was not sufficiently responding to her engagement on my own posts. Since then, I have worked harder to live up to my own ideal of engaging twice on posts published by anyone who likes or comments on my posts. It's harder than it sounds and has meant a reduction in my posts simply because of the time involved. (I wrote a post about this on the next page which performed quite well and I hope served as an apology to the connection concerned, although of course she was not named.)

This 2:1 reciprocal formula is one way to engage. Another was developed by UK florist Kate Lister who takes a wonderfully irreverent approach to LinkedIn. She operates on a 5:1 ratio of commenting on other's posts to comments received on hers. That is definitely a giving approach although Kate stands to gain, too. Each time she comments on someone else's post, her photo appears in the newsfeed for the poster and their audience to see, thereby exposing Kate to a different audience. Following this logic, it is an excellent idea to engage with as large a number of 1st- and 2nd-degree connections' posts as possible to widen your sphere of influence and share the love.

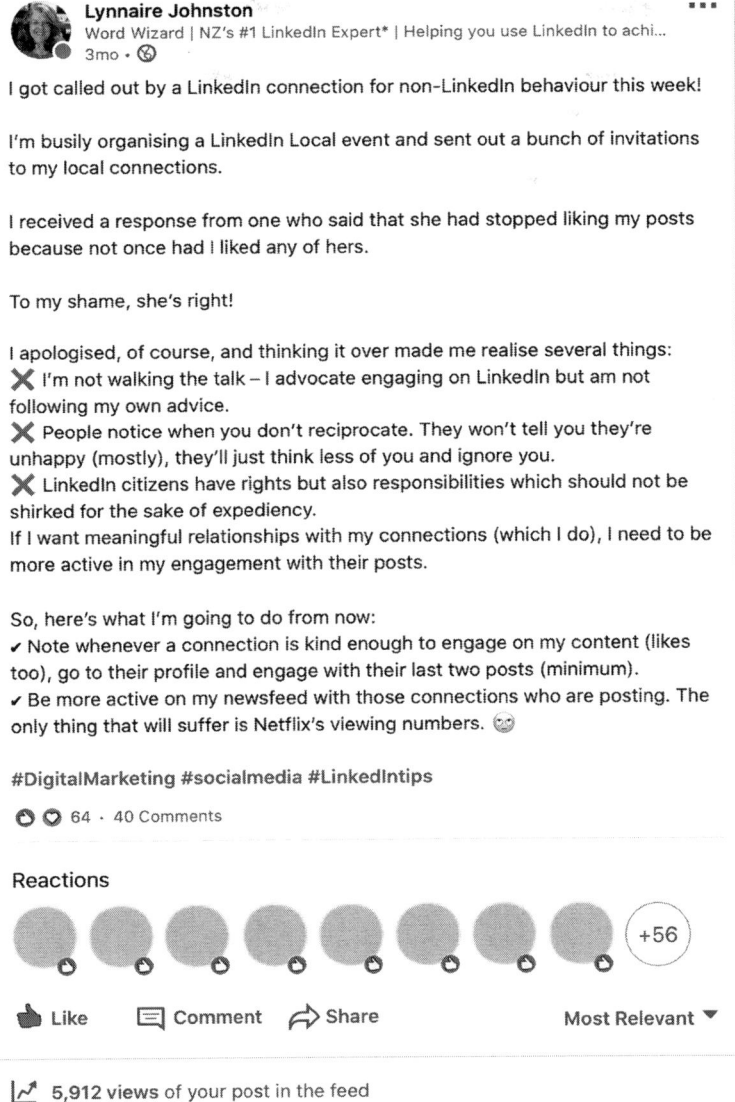

Lynnaire Johnston
Word Wizard | NZ's #1 LinkedIn Expert* | Helping you use LinkedIn to achi...
3mo · 🌐

I got called out by a LinkedIn connection for non-LinkedIn behaviour this week!

I'm busily organising a LinkedIn Local event and sent out a bunch of invitations to my local connections.

I received a response from one who said that she had stopped liking my posts because not once had I liked any of hers.

To my shame, she's right!

I apologised, of course, and thinking it over made me realise several things:
✖ I'm not walking the talk – I advocate engaging on LinkedIn but am not following my own advice.
✖ People notice when you don't reciprocate. They won't tell you they're unhappy (mostly), they'll just think less of you and ignore you.
✖ LinkedIn citizens have rights but also responsibilities which should not be shirked for the sake of expediency.
If I want meaningful relationships with my connections (which I do), I need to be more active in my engagement with their posts.

So, here's what I'm going to do from now:
✔ Note whenever a connection is kind enough to engage on my content (likes too), go to their profile and engage with their last two posts (minimum).
✔ Be more active on my newsfeed with those connections who are posting. The only thing that will suffer is Netflix's viewing numbers. 😳

#DigitalMarketing #socialmedia #LinkedIntips

👍❤ 64 · 40 Comments

Reactions

+56

👍 Like   💬 Comment   ↪ Share   Most Relevant ▼

📈 5,912 views of your post in the feed

In this post I shared an insight gleaned from a comment made by a connection.

When to use engaging as a strategy

When there is a constant stream of posts to choose from in the newsfeed, engaging is an excellent strategy. But it requires a decent sized network of connections – 1000 or more. Fewer and there is a risk of not being seen in the wider network and noticed by others.

One solution is to search for topics using hashtags, but the popularity of specific hashtags waxes and wanes so research the most popular in your industry for greatest reach.

A second solution is to search for high-flyers in your industry who have big networks and are active on the platform. When they post on subjects you can legitimately comment on, make sure you do.

Another reason to use comment marketing as a strategy (the hashtag #strategy itself has more than five million followers) is when creating content yourself is difficult. Not everyone has the resources – time, ability, interest – to consistently produce posts and articles, but most of us can cogently write two or three sentences on a topic that is in our area of expertise. And that's all comment marketing is.

Top engagement tips

1. Commenting is the most valuable form of engagement.

Commenting on another person's post makes you a good LinkedIn citizen, gets you noticed by other people and depending on what you write, demonstrates your own knowledge of the topic under discussion.

2. Hijacking posts is frowned on.

Making comments unrelated to the post and pushing your own barrow will not endear you to other LinkedIn members. By all means add to the conversation but not at the expense of the original poster.

3. Sharing doesn't work. Except when it does.

It is generally thought that the algorithm doesn't promote shared posts very widely but a colleague of ours netted well over 250,000 views on a shared post. The original poster received nothing like that number. Such success is, however, rare.

4. When commenting, make an effort.

A comment that reads "great post" is a poor comment which wastes your time and that of the poster because it doesn't add to the conversation. Instead, ask a question or express your opinion. LinkedIn is one platform where it's ok to disagree with someone provided you do so politely.

5. If someone tries to derail your post, delete their comment.

A post's author can control a number of aspects of the comments including removing any @mention (or tag), reporting it and deleting it.

6. Unhappy with a comment you've posted? Change it.

It's easy to edit a comment, just as you can change a published post. Click on the icon on the top right of the comment which indicates how long ago you wrote it (e.g. 21 hours) choose the editing pen, make your changes and save them.

7. Vary the style of likes given.

LinkedIn offers six variations on liking a post – the usual blue thumbs-up, hands clapping (applause or congratulations), a hand holding a heart (support), a heart (love), a lightbulb (insightful) and a questioning face (curious). Any of these is counted as a like, and they display alongside the person's face under Reactions immediately below the post.

8. View comments by Most Relevant or Most Recent.

By default, the algorithm ranks what it sees as the Most Relevant comments first but to look at the thread in chronological order, choose Most Recent.

9. Connect with generous commenters.

When you spot someone who's regularly commenting on posts you're interested in, invite them to connect if it's appropriate. You can then respond in kind to each other's posts which benefits you both.

LinkedIn by the numbers

- 50% of LinkedIn users say they are more likely to buy from a company they interact with on the platform.

- More than 50% of all social traffic to B2B websites and blogs comes from LinkedIn.

- 65% of B2B companies have acquired a customer through LinkedIn.

- 80% of B2B leads come from LinkedIn vs. 13% on Twitter and 7% on Facebook.

Sources: foundationinc.co/

Summary

Comment marketing, as described here, is a legitimate way to be noticed on LinkedIn. In fact, it is woven into the very fabric of the platform but is an aspect of LinkedIn marketing which is not used effectively or strategically by many people. When you conscientiously and regularly comment on another member's posts, you will be more visible and more highly regarded. Even a small level of engagement will enhance your presence on the platform and result in more invitations to connect.

Checklist

My post	
Did it provide opportunity for comments?	
Have I replied to all comments?	
Connections' posts	
Have I liked the post?	
Did I/could I use a different reaction than like?	
Have I commented?	
Did my comment add value?	
Did I tag the poster so that they received a notification of my comment?	
Did I check back to see if the poster replied to my comment and write a reply if needed?	

Direct messaging

Building strong relationships

In this chapter:

COMMUNICATION is fundamental to humans. We need it to foster cooperation, to get things done, and in business, to persuade others to buy. It's crucially important and regularly misused. Communication is also fundamental on LinkedIn where all activity centres around it.

LinkedIn allows members to communicate with each other via direct messaging and anyone can freely message their 1st-degree connections. This is yet another reason why it is useful to have a strong network on the platform – personal access to more people.

Direct messages are excellent for bypassing gatekeepers and reaching your intended recipient. It does, however, require recipients to monitor their messages but with the importance of LinkedIn now widely understood, it is increasingly rare for messages to go unseen.

While email is enjoying a resurgence, I believe that direct messaging via LinkedIn is a better option. Most people manage their own LinkedIn account and receive message notifications, and messages don't get dumped into junk or spam folders as often happens with emails. It also resolves the issue of people using Reply All with emails, or messages going to unintended recipients.

A further reason to consider using LinkedIn direct messages is the variety of ways it can be used. Options include text, voice and video. The message function also includes locations and calendars, plus the ability to include files of many kinds. Most of us use only a fraction of these features.

A LinkedIn direct message is still sufficiently unusual, so stands out. Permission to send is unnecessary and opening it won't install malware on the recipient's computer – all great reasons to use LinkedIn messaging.

I strongly believe in the power of direct messaging and use it constantly in my own and my clients' LinkedIn marketing. Not only is it useful for transactional messages ('let's organise a time to chat'), but also for sending someone a question ('I'm stuck on xxx, please can you help me resolve this?') or building a relationship by asking them to explain a bit about what they do or an aspect of their profile you want clarification on.

Direct messaging can also be used to:

- Thank a new connection for having accepted your invitation. (This is especially effective when you send a voice or video message. See chapter 1.)

- Invite a connection to an event or meeting.

- Request participation in a survey.

- Ask for help with a project you're working on.

- Share information you think would be useful.

- Persuade a connection to visit your website or landing page.

Direct messaging nuts and bolts

On **desktop**, the messaging function can be found under Messaging on the main menu at the top of the screen or by clicking on the black Messaging box at the bottom right of the screen. On **mobile** the speech bubble icon indicating messages is at the top right of the LinkedIn app Home page where a number inside a red circle indicates unread messages.

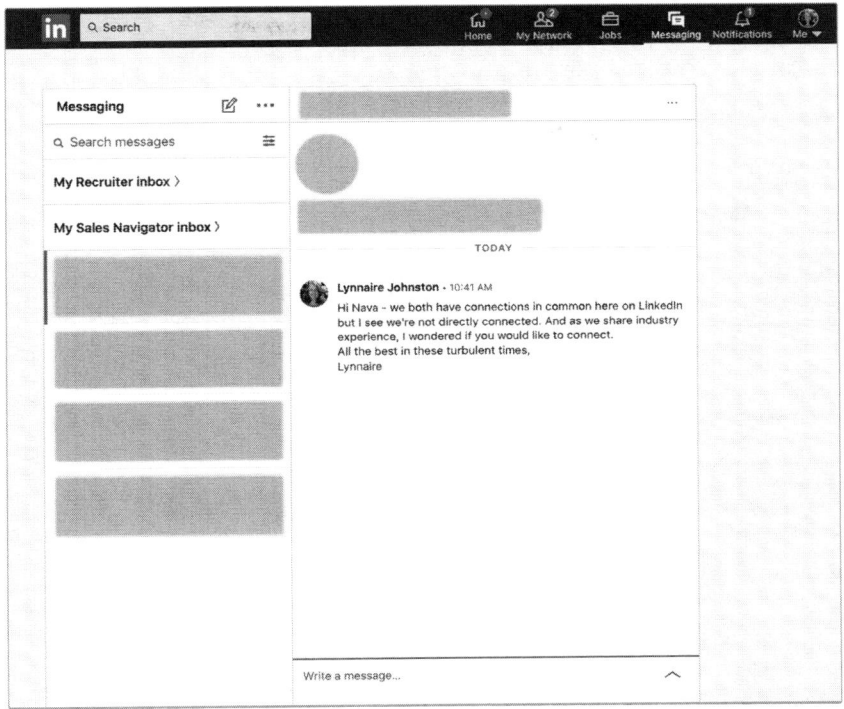

The messaging section can be found under the Messaging tab in the top menu.

At the time of writing, only 1st-degree connections can be messaged from a free account. However, paid accounts such as Sales Navigator make it much easier. Sales Navigator has its own messaging system, InMail, which has the added benefit of allowing those who are not 1st-degree connections to message each other.

Should you want to send a message to a certain group or subset of connections, you will need to conduct a search so you know who to send to. Searches are possible on both free and paid LinkedIn accounts and filters are used to help find those who most closely fit the parameters you want.

These filters include:

- 1st- or 2nd-degree connections
- Location
- Current company
- Past companies
- Industries
- Profile language
- Schools
- Services
- Name

Sales Navigator offers more filters and the ability for searches to be saved.

Depending on the purpose of your message and the number of recipients, a solution is to create a group message. This is similar to a group email message, where all participants receive the same message with one push of the send button.

Creating direct messages

LinkedIn provides three methods by which we can send messages – voice, video and text. And messaging couldn't be simpler.

- On **desktop**, go to Messaging in the main menu.
- Click the blue editing pen and type in the name or names of your recipients.
- Write a message. You can add files, gifs, photos and emojis.
- Click the blue Send button to send your message.

On **mobile** it is just as simple but with more options although these are semi-hidden behind the + key to the left of the Write a message box.

- The messaging tab on mobile is on the top of your screen to the right of the search box on the Home page.

- To send a message, click on the blue editing pen circle at the top of the screen, and type in the name of your recipient/s.

- On the left of the Write a message box is the + key. Tap this to bring up a menu containing Attachment, Photos, Camera, Video, GIF, Location, Availability and Mention. This last feature allows you to add another recipient to your message.

Most of these options will be self-explanatory but the more unusual ones offer functions you might not have thought of using:

- GIF – LinkedIn offers quite a selection of different GIFs but I would advise caution as this isn't Facebook. None of the offerings are potentially offensive but they aren't business oriented so it would pay to know your recipient. LinkedIn is primarily about business relationships, after all.

- Location – this sends a location and potentially your current one without seeming to check that you want to send it. Caution advised.

- Availability – takes you to your calendar from which you can choose a day/time, telling your recipient, 'These are the times that work for me'. This isn't sent automatically.

- Mention – brings up the @ allowing you to add another recipient to the message. Why you wouldn't include the person at the message invite stage, I'm not sure but it does provide another option.

- Video and Camera – these take you direct to those functions on your phone or tablet which you can then add to your message before sending. (More on video messaging shortly.)

Voice messages

Of these features, the one I use most often is voice message. This shows up as a microphone icon to the right of the Write a message box when you've chosen your recipient. Tap the icon and a big blue microphone appears on the screen. Hold this down and record your message. When you've finished, lift your finger and either send the message or delete it. At any point in the process you can swipe right to delete it and start again.

The microphone icon from where you can send voice messages to connections. This is available only on the app.

The voice message feature allows you to record one message at a time. There are apps available that allow bulk batching of messages but I highly recommend staying well away from them. LinkedIn is diligent in fighting external automation platforms which seek to destroy the relationship-building aspect of the platform and in its Terms and Conditions explicitly prohibits them.

Voice messages can be up to a minute long so there's no time to waffle. Prepare what to say before starting to record to avoid mistakes because – and this seems a shame – it's not possible to listen to the message before sending. My advice: if you're not sure you're happy with it, don't send it. Re-record it. But the contrary view here is that it should sound natural. You don't want to appear rehearsed. After all, one of the reasons for sending a voice message is to build or cement a personal relationship with your connection.

Since voice messaging became available in 2018, I've been using it regularly to nurture relationships with new connections. Any time someone new connects, I send them a voice message. In only one case has anyone been negative about this. An Auckland strategist whose profile says she is passionate about leadership but who in her communication to me said she found 'messages like this' inappropriate. It was unclear whether she disliked the content of the message (which thanked her for connecting) or the idea of the voice message itself. Her response read:

> 'These messages i [sic] do find inappropriate and respond to simple requests to link [sic] only.'

People often don't know voice messaging is available and ask how it's done, so they can try it for themselves. However, voice messages can only be sent to 1st-degree connections.

Video and video messaging

It is also possible to send video messages through the mobile app. Like voice messages, each one is unique to the recipient. Bulk recording and sending is not an option.

Video, however, can be used to record a single message off the LinkedIn platform which can be sent to many. Of course, that precludes any personalisation, reducing the effectiveness of your efforts.

I like recording messages using someone's name, so the recipient knows it was just for them. There seems something karmic about it that prompts a positive response. But it may be that the uniqueness of a video message outweighs the personalisation of a voice message. The only way to be sure is to try it. And that, like many things on LinkedIn, is a very good thing to do.

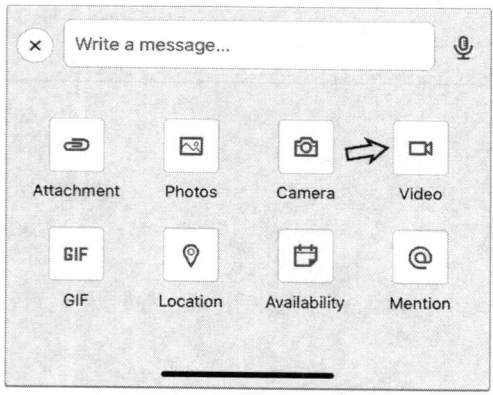

Video messaging and other options can be found under messaging on the app.

Ways to use direct messages

The options for using the direct message function are as varied as the people using them. For me, a voice message is a great way to say 'thank you for connecting' when someone has accepted my connection invite or asked me to connect. It works remarkably well; recipients respond positively and more consistently than they do to a simple written message. It seems somehow to resonate, to make an impact. (I explain this in greater detail in Chapter 1.) This screen-shot below is an example of a great follow-up message.

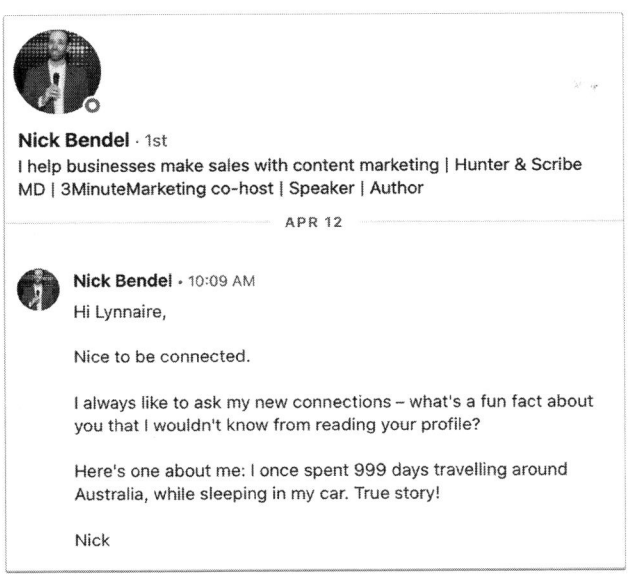

Example of a great connection message.

I also send direct messages to my connections each month with value-added material that helps them with their LinkedIn market-ing. But equally, I could send info about my other area of expertise, copywriting. The key words here are 'value-added'. Sending spam messages is inappropriate if you are coming from a sharing and giv-ing angle on LinkedIn.

In the course of research for this book, I canvassed colleagues on how they use direct messaging in their LinkedIn marketing. Here are some of their methods:

• Sending a survey that acts as lead generation tool.

- Asking a question aimed at determining if a new connection might be interested in the products and services being offered.

- Asking a question that begins building a relationship or is related to the person's line of work.

- Commenting on a common situation and asking, genuinely, how they are doing (as in during the coronavirus pandemic).

- Introducing connections to each other to facilitate networking.

Before the coronavirus pandemic it was common for people to request in-person meetings with those they had 'met' only online. Direct messages suggesting a coffee were an effective way to achieve that. In light of the virus, how we meet has changed and we now get together using Zoom or Skype. Again, direct messages are an ideal way to move the relationship forward.

But these uses of this endlessly adaptable feature are just a few examples of what's possible. Start thinking about how it could help your business or career and you'll be surprised at the ideas that spring to mind.

Direct messaging results

Whether your direct messaging efforts are a success will depend on the quality of your communications. Here are some of the types of responses you might receive:

- An acknowledgement of your message through a comment or an emoji.

- An enquiry about your product or service.

- A personalised message.

- One of the prompted messages.

- A voice message.

- A video message.

However, inevitably not everyone you message will respond. In fact, it would have to be a very attractive offer indeed or a very small recipient sample to achieve a 100% success rate. Still, response rates are much higher in my experience than conventional emails. Although I concede there is room for both and I will often move a message thread to email if it looks to be ongoing, simply so I can better track the messages.

At the early stage of the conversation with someone you have only recently met on LinkedIn, trust levels are low, and one party may be keener on the interaction than the other. The aim is to develop the relationship in a way that isn't threatening and that adds value for both parties. For instance, asking what the person you're messaging does is a waste of an opportunity. If you're communicating with them, you should already know this and a bit about them, who they've worked for and where they're located.

Don't, however, make the mistake of thinking that no reply means the recipient has either not received the message or has ignored it. The message may simply have slipped down their feed (like emails do in your inbox) and been overlooked. I've been surprised how often a conversation that seemed to stop dead in its tracks gets picked back up again weeks or even months later. Then it's a scramble to look up the original thread and get back up to speed on the person.

If you are having multiple conversations simultaneously on LinkedIn, it can be difficult to keep track. Sometimes messages get lost in the messaging app simply through sheer volume.

To a LinkedIn giver who wants to communicate, but not at a level considered spam, direct messaging is a godsend. It is a low-key way to reach exactly the right person. Do it right and the relationships will come. Also keep in mind that the more you develop these relationships, the more people will be keen to interact with you in other ways. For instance, they will engage with your posts, furthering your reach. Your name will be top of mind should they be asked if they know someone providing your product or service. They may be keen to give you a LinkedIn recommendation or endorsement. Or, they may recommend you for a podcast or other media opportunity. The possibilities are endless because you don't know what or who your connection knows and they might be able to provide the exact opportunities you're looking for.

Message frequency

How often to send direct messages is a tricky question and the answer is 'it depends'.

When you are engaged in a conversation, respond within as reasonable a time as you can but don't expect the other person to be waiting on your every word.

When sending a campaign of some kind to selected connections, be judicious in your frequency. Once a month is probably sufficient but don't pack the message full of spammy, salesy material. Make it informational and value-added so it is consistent with your other activities such as personalised messaging and non-promotional posts. This may be perceived as peculiar by those who prefer a more sales-focused approach and who are not interested in building and nurturing a relationship. They want a far faster method of selling that bombards connections with offers, messages of dubious value and a hard sell. To my mind, that ruins relationships rather than nurtures them. And it's one reason why I always turn down connection invite messages from a particular industry aligned with my own as I know the moment I accept, I'll be in for a barrage of unwanted messages.

My strategy instead is to be low key; sending often enough to remain on the radar but not so frequently that I am perceived as pestering them. If six months or so go by with no response from the person, I simply remove them from the list. I don't disconnect, just no longer message them. I don't do so within this time because it generally takes a number of touches for people to respond. And, if they decide they do need my service after I've stopped messaging them, I hope they will remember those messages AND my name.

And so, in answer to the question at the top of this section: how often should you direct message someone, the answer is most likely to be somewhere in the three to five-week range, depending on what you're sending and your objective.

LinkedIn in Action

A Melbourne design company specialising in the community health field, wanted to develop closer bonds with other people and organisations in its niche. It decided to direct message all its LinkedIn connections based in the local area and see who was open to meeting for coffee.

While the percentage of acceptances wasn't high, those who agreed were fully engaged with the networking process. The business owner found herself with introductions to other businesses which in turn meant a larger network and more opportunities to talk about her work with others who might have need of her services. A bonus was a wider network she could call on when she needed professional services for her business.

• • •

A Sydney-based business publishing entrepreneur has built an entire business on LinkedIn. Using LinkedIn as her sole marketing avenue, she has grown her business from a standing start to over six figures in under three years. Any business owner, consultant, director seeking to write, publish and market their book approaches her first. She has achieved this by a multi-pronged approach, one of which is to direct message new connections with a survey to find out if they are interested in her services. This is done very subtly and those who respond positively receive follow-up messages designed to take the conversation to the next level. This approach allows her to weed out those who are uninterested in her service and instead concentrate on those who are.

What NOT to send in messages

For many months, my regular message to connections was accompanied by a PDF. However, I failed to take into account that many people look at their messages on smaller screens than desktops, making a PDF too small to read. When a colleague kindly pointed this out, I immediately ceased sending PDFs. Now, I create a web page for the information and add the link to my message instead of attaching a PDF. It has the advantage of being more visually attractive because it shows a preview of the web page. It also provides reassurance that the site you're sending people to is legitimate and, if you are sending these in bulk, they are often quicker to send.

I am most grateful to my connection for pointing this out. But it serves as yet another example of how important it is to have good relationships with other professionals who have your back. And, of course, to be there for them should an occasion arise. And if it doesn't, pay it forward. As the great Seth Godin says:

> 'I'm not teaching people selfish secrets, I'm teaching them generous principles and if they can pay them forward, I don't want any credit. I just want to see things get better.'

As mentioned in the previous section, direct messages that could be considered spam are best avoided. Make them useful and add value by sharing information the receiver may not know. This has the added bonus of making you appear knowledgeable and of being someone who is willing to give without expectation of reward.

Getting it done!

Direct messaging a large group of connections takes time (i.e. money) so it's worth doing well and the best way to achieve that is to plan. I'm not talking about long-winded, multi-page plans that take forever to put together and then sit in a bottom drawer. I'm talking about a clear and organised strategy that consistently moves you toward your goals. In my case, for instance, I want to be seen as a LinkedIn expert, the person to go to when LinkedIn work needs to be done. This means I need to share useful information with my connections, where possible taking them with me on my LinkedIn journey so they learn, too. To do this, I need to prove my value and there's no better way than helping them to achieve their own goals on the platform.

I favour the type of planning that can be easily changed should something else come along (as happened in early 2020 when Covid-19 overturned all our lives) but at the very least a 12-month or 10–15 message sequence should be worked out. This planning will mean that the messages are more likely to be sent because they can be added to the organisation's content marketing plan.

Being ad hoc with direct messaging isn't as effective as being consistent. Consistency results in recipients getting to know you and welcoming your messages because they have value.

Responding to direct messages

I've talked quite a bit about sending direct messages, and a discussion about receiving them is also useful starting with etiquette. This dictates that when replying to a direct message you should always be polite, even if you are not interested in the person or their product or service.

Take this message I received in response to sending free, and I'd like to think useful, information to a connection:

just stop

you ain't making me money ~ pass me a good lead or bounce

Now, the lack of punctuation notwithstanding, that is wrong on so many levels. First, there was no attempt to be polite. No 'please don't send me messages like this'. It is unusual for people to respond in this way because most are exceedingly polite even when they're not interested. But every now and again someone like this young man – who is in car sales – decides there is no mileage in being polite. And the relationship breaks down.

His attitude is a mistake because with an online profile, there is no off duty. You are always representing the company you work for, which means that offensive comments like this young man's also reflect poorly on his employer. He also seemed to forget or be unaware that LinkedIn is about building relationships and I rather suspect that, if asked, he would complain that LinkedIn doesn't work for him.

But most people are not so rude and ask politely not to receive messages anymore. This should always be respected and responded to in the same vein.

The other aspect of receiving messages that is important is a timely reply when a response is appropriate or expected. When a connection messages you, they expect you to respond in the same timeframe as they would an email. Delays can look impolite. But here's the rub. If you are sending and receiving multiple messages, they may get lost in the message feed (I know mine do so I have someone help keep me on the straight and narrow). The solution to this is to check your unread messages on a regular basis so you don't miss them.

If you receive multiple messages that require the same or a standard answer, have these written and saved where you can easily get at them. Sticky Notes on Windows and Stickies on Mac are both helpful for this or use Trello boards – whatever productivity app you use daily.

Top direct messaging tips

1. Use the direct message option to reach out.

While direct messages on LinkedIn are increasing in popularity and use, they have still not reached critical mass. If you want to personally reach out to a connection but don't have their personal email address, send them a DM instead.

2. Don't use direct messages to spam connections.

This is considered very poor form. Just because you don't legally need their permission to contact them for marketing purposes (like you do with emails), doesn't mean you should abuse the privilege.

3. Use the forwarding function to message the same attachment to multiple people.

The LinkedIn messaging feature is very basic and annoying to use because messages get lost in the stream. But if you are sending the same document to many people it's easy to forward it instead of having to attach it to each message.

4. Instead of sending a document, send a link.

Documents don't display well on small devices so offer an alternative to your PDF – a link. Still send the PDF if you wish, but you may find the link is more regularly opened than the attachment.

LinkedIn by the numbers

- LinkedIn generates three times more visitor-to-lead conversions than Twitter and Facebook. Not only do more potential leads land on your website through LinkedIn, they're also more qualified and willing to buy.

- 79% of B2B marketers see LinkedIn as a good source for generating leads.

- 46% of social traffic to corporate websites comes from LinkedIn.

- LinkedIn is the top place to find quality content according to 91% of marketing executives. Other social media platforms were down in the 20s.

Sources: LinkedIn, foundationinc.co

Summary

Direct messaging via LinkedIn is a relatively new form of marketing to potential clients which offers the advantage of being different. Using this technique well demonstrates you are committed to communicating and sharing material of value, without expectation of reward. In this chapter I have covered who to direct message, the different methods of direct messaging available, ways to use direct messages and the results you can expect. I have also looked at message frequency, what not to send in messages, responding to direct messaging and, finally, planning and implementing your messaging campaigns. If you have mastered these basics you are now ready to begin pulling together the different LinkedIn activities in a cohesive strategy that will get you the results you want. And that is what Chapter 5 covers.

Checklist

Direct messaging plan template

Month	Jan	Feb	Mar	Apr	May
Target market					
Topic					
Start send date					
Material source					
Other marketing to consider					
Images/videos required – source, delivery date					

5

Harnessing the 4 strategies for success

In this chapter:

IN PREVIOUS CHAPTERS, I discussed the different strategies available for LinkedIn marketing: connecting, engaging, publishing and direct messaging. This chapter pulls together that knowledge to help you decide how to use it because even the best ideas in the world won't succeed unless put into action. This chapter explains how to get your LinkedIn marketing strategy up and running, including how to handle potential obstacles.

Matching strategies with objectives

The first step in developing a strategy is to understand your objectives and to be clear on the goals you are trying to achieve. Here are some of the most common (a longer list can be found in Appendix 1):

- Changing career or moving up the ladder in your current industry.

- Exposure in the media through podcasts or online articles.

- Being offered speaking opportunities.

- Attracting capability or project partners.

- Widening your network of trusted advisors.

- Being seen as an industry expert, thought leader or influencer.

- Bringing in new clients to your business or company.

- Sharing knowledge and information that might not be found elsewhere.

You might want to do several of these things or something else entirely.

But whatever your motivation for wanting to use LinkedIn – the best social media platform for business – as part of your marketing efforts, you will likely need or want to do one or more of the following:

- Become visible
- Build authority
- Develop your brand
- Create trust
- Promote yourself or your organisation
- Promote others
- Create controversy
- Entertain
- Gain industry expert status
- Engage with others

To achieve the goals you have in mind, they need to be matched with the correct strategy or combination of strategies. Not all strategies will be useful in your circumstances and even those that are may not be useful all the time.

To achieve your goals you will need a strategy, a champion and a plan, most likely a content plan. You will also need patience. A worthwhile LinkedIn strategy could take several months before its full impact is felt. While it's a good idea to react to changing situations during that time and adapt where necessary in response, the decision to dedicate time and other resources to this needs to be firm. LinkedIn is about farming, not hunting and those expecting to make a quick buck from the platform will be in for disappointment unless they go about it the right way – with motivation, commitment and the right strategy.

Where to start

When planning a LinkedIn campaign for an organisation, you will need committed buy-in from those in authority in your organisation. A 'maybe we'll do a post a week if we get around to it' attitude won't be enough to make a difference. Instead, a commitment to posting high quality content on a regular, if not frequent basis, is required. And, if you are intending to use LinkedIn for yourself rather than the organisation you work for, that decision to commit is on you. I have seen many otherwise great LinkedIn plans go south because the organisation or person behind the campaign gave up before they had a chance to make an impact.

While on the subject of LinkedIn for organisations, you will need a champion who understands the value that using LinkedIn can bring to the organisation. You will need someone who sees that the platform can be used to differentiate the company from its competitors, and who knows it's important for gaining credibility, building trust and being seen as the go-to organisation in your industry. This person should be in charge of ensuring that the agreed upon LinkedIn strategy is implemented.

Once you have the commitment and a champion, you will need a plan. The plan should identify the LinkedIn strategies you intend to use and the content that will form the backbone of these strategies. You will need someone sufficiently experienced to carry it out. This will help you organise your posts, decide on suitable content that meets the strategy's goals and encourage engagement that will get the posts noticed. It will also make sure you are using all the posting options available on the platform and, by measuring the results, check you remain on track.

Resources – what you'll need

A LinkedIn campaign or programme such as the ones proposed in this book requires resources. Resources such as time, writing capability, videos or the ability to record them, content or shareable information and, if you decide to outsource some or most of this – money. (It is unwise to outsource everything.) The work that goes into developing a strong LinkedIn presence that helps you reach your goals is not insignificant. In fact, you could work on it all day, every day and still not do everything possible.

Some people claim you can spend 15 minutes a day on LinkedIn and be effective. I don't share that belief. Instead, if you understand that LinkedIn is THE place to be on social media for your business, it is worth spending the time and effort required to make a difference. Least effort will bring you fewest rewards. Instead, decide on your LinkedIn priorities and concentrate on those. Once you have them working effectively, move on to the next strategy while maintaining your efforts with the existing ones. For instance, if your profile isn't the best it could be, start there. All other LinkedIn strategies are based on you having a complete, well-thought-out and eye-catching profile. If you are not convinced yours fits the bill, check out my e-book at wordwizard.co.nz/book-resources because you do not want people looking at a less than optimal profile. You will be judged on this so make it the best you possibly can.

Deciding to increase your connection numbers, especially if they are fewer than 1000, will likely be high on your list of priorities (in fact, I contend it should be second behind creating a great profile.) As discussed in Chapter 1 – Connecting – you want as many good quality connections as possible. But it takes time. LinkedIn has an accepted limit of 75 invites a day, although there's plenty of evidence to suggest that more can be sent without any negative effect. Just make sure that the connection invites in your Message Sent folder (LinkedIn.com/mynetwork/invitation-manager/sent/) are no more than three to four weeks old and there aren't thousands of them. A huge list of outstanding invitations indicates to LinkedIn that those you are trying to connect with are not interested, which may flag your profile as contravening the platform's Terms and Conditions.

The use of automation to send connection invites is increasingly common. However, I am not an advocate as I believe automation is contrary to the values and philosophy of LinkedIn. The organisation devotes massive resources to stop it and there are countless incidences of accounts being shut down because profile holders have been actively using automation. Furthermore, the use of automation contravenes LinkedIn's Terms and Conditions.

Returning to the subject of resources, let's turn our attention to content. Most of the strategies mentioned here need large quantities of good quality content. This can come from three places:

- A large library of existing content.

- The resources to write or create it.

- Outsourcing to someone who understands the principles of LinkedIn, knows what you are trying to do and can provide content that showcases you and your business in a way that reflects your professionalism and standing in the industry.

As we have already discussed, the strategy of merely inserting links from an external blog or website into a LinkedIn post is pointless and injurious to your business reputation. At the very least you look lazy and ignorant of how LinkedIn works. No professional or organisation wants to have that thought about them.

Deciding on the best strategy for your business

Having read this far in the book, you will have already formed some opinions on what might work best for you. While it isn't quite as clear cut as this, the basic premise is to match your desired objective with the LinkedIn strategy or strategies that will best help you achieve it. For instance, if you wish to become seen as a thought leader, regularly publishing high-quality content that presents your ideas in a compelling way is an excellent strategy. But you can see that expecting to achieve the same result by employing an engagement strategy in isolation would not be nearly as effective.

To a certain extent, strategies need to build on each other. Start with a quality profile (as mentioned on more than one previous occasion!) followed by actively increasing connection numbers. Then, once those connections reach a certain level, there will be value in creating content, as you will have sufficient connections and followers who see it to make the effort worthwhile. There is little point in spending time creating excellent content if only a few people are going to read it.

Let's return then to the most common objectives (remembering you can have more than one).

1. Generate leads (always at the top of everyone's list, no matter what they tell you).

2. Develop a reputation as a thought leader.

3. Be seen as the go-to person in an industry. (This and the previous point, while similar, are not the same).

4. Create a wide network of connections for any number of purposes.

5. Meet industry heavyweights who can help you with your career/business (consciously or unconsciously).

6. Promote a book, TV series, podcast or other media.

7. Seek invitations from the media to be in a TV series, a guest on a podcast or to write articles in prestigious publications.

8. Find a new job or move up the career leader. (Not just a matter of having a quality LinkedIn profile.)

9. Create and develop a group of supporters who can provide advice and assistance in any number of ways.

10. Build your personal or business brand.

11. Learn from others who share their knowledge or information on relevant innovations and updates. LinkedIn is a goldmine of information.

12. Build trust through recommendations.

13. Find potential distributors, partners and service providers.

And these are not the only reasons. But whatever you are trying to do professionally, LinkedIn can help you get there through a combination of any one of the strategies listed in this book:

- Connecting

- Engaging

- Publishing

- Direct messaging

All these strategies need a fully complete and optimised profile and, where relevant, company page.

So, let's match each objective with possible strategies and see how that might look.

(It is assumed that you have a top-quality LinkedIn profile. If not, go back and complete that first. Use my free guide at wordwizard. co.nz/book-resources if you like.)

These are suggested strategies, not rules you must follow.

Objective	Strategies	Rationale
Lead generation	Connecting, posting and direct messaging	Lead generation requires a large pool of potential clients or customers, so having a strong network is crucial. Back this with regular posting to demonstrate your knowledge and nurture your leads with value-added direct messages. Promote your business only rarely.
Thought leadership	Connecting and posting	A big audience is needed for your ideas to be widely shared, and using all five posting options plus writing articles is the way to do it.
Industry leader	Connecting and posting	Connect widely but outside your industry, with those who use the products or services you provide. Share plenty of useful, unique and ultra-specific information they cannot get elsewhere.
Network creation	Connecting and engaging	Connect widely, inside and outside your industry then engage with your connections' activity (posts, comments).

Objective	Strategies	Rationale
Meeting industry heavyweights	Connecting and engaging	Connect personally with those you wish to get to know with a unique connection message, asking how you might be of service. Engage often and compellingly with their content.
Promotion of products or services	Connecting, posting and direct messaging	Connect with potential customers and clients, post valuable and useful content (only rarely promoting your products or services), offer free info either by publishing or direct messaging, or both.
Media invitations	Connecting, posting and engaging	Connect with media representatives, podcasters and writers who may be in a position to promote you and your brand.
Job hunting	Connecting and engaging	Connect with recruiters and those you would like to work for. Engage with the content of those individuals and their company pages where relevant.
Moving up the career ladder or changing industries	Connecting, engaging and posting	Connect with heavyweights in the industry you want to move into. Nurture them, engage with their posts and develop personal relationships if you can. Publish content that demonstrates your knowledge of the industry you're keen to join.

Objective	Strategies	Rationale
Supporters network	Connecting, engaging and direct messaging	Develop a group of supporters, also known as your tribe. These might be all in one group or they might be separate from each other and have an individual relationship with you. Direct messaging is imperative here, the 1-2-1 kind.
Brand building	Connecting, engaging, posting and direct messaging	To build a brand on LinkedIn you will need to employ every opportunity and feature there is, including posting and engaging from your company page.
Learning	Connecting and engaging	The wider your network of relevant people, the more interesting will be the information in your newsfeed. The more you engage with the most relevant posts, the more LinkedIn will put those posts in your newsfeed.
Credibility building	Connecting, engaging and posting	This is a slow process of connecting with the right people, engaging with their activity and publishing your own material that enhances your standing in your industry.

Objective	Strategies	Rationale
Trust building	Connecting, engaging and posting	Developed slowly, trust can be damaged irreparably in a moment of inattention. If you do something stupid (we've all been there), fix it immediately. Take down the post, delete the comment or whatever you need to rectify the situation. If the mistake occurred in a direct message, apologise profusely and do something kind for the person, such as giving them an endorsement, a recommendation or @mention in a post.
Finding distributors, partners and service providers	Connecting and direct messaging	Carefully target those you might want to work with, and those similar to them so you develop a wide network. Depending on your industry and what you require from these people, you might be able to go straight from connecting to direct messaging.

The strategies in action

The following scenarios are aimed at showing how with a small tweak here and more emphasis on a certain activity there it is possible to achieve excellent results.

Scenario 1 (Relationship building)

You own a small one-person business you are keen to grow. Your business is in the B2B sector, providing products or services to other businesses. Your plan is to use LinkedIn to become better known in your industry, to stand out from other similar providers and to develop relationships with potential clients. Here's a potential strategy to adopt:

- **Connecting** – Search for, find and connect with as many members of your target market as you can find. Send a personalised connection message; the more specific to them (based on their profile), the better.

- **Engaging** – When sending your 'thank you for connecting' message, attempt a conversation. This could be a question, a comment on what you have in common, or offering some genuinely useful material (but don't come across as spammy – ask yourself if you would want to receive this from someone you had only just 'met'). Keep an eye on your notifications and when one of your connections publishes a good quality post, engage with it. Start a discussion, share your opinion, add value from your experience.

- **Posting** – Begin posting value-added material on LinkedIn on a regular and frequent basis, 2–3 times a week. Choose a mix of text, image and video posts. Seek engagement for posts during their first 60-minutes to improve reach.

- **Direct messaging** – Send direct messages to people engaging on your posts to thank them for their interaction and invite them to connect or, if they are connections, attempt to initiate a conversation. Use this as another vehicle to build relationships.

Scenario 2 (Encouraging engagement)

You run a member organisation with national reach and thousands of committed members. However, your LinkedIn efforts, while consistent, receive very little traction or reach. You are posting links only with little or no accompanying text and do not attempt to engage.

Your objective is to use LinkedIn to create greater interest in the organisation by achieving higher readership of your posts.

Here's a simple strategy to adopt:

- **Connecting** – Send a personalised message to any of the organisation's members not already connected with you.

- **Posting** – Abandon the practice of only uploading links and instead post content directly into the post so that it can be read by LinkedIn members within the platform. Write posts that encourage engagement.

- **Engaging** – Respond to those who comment on posts to increase the number of people who will see your material.

Scenario 3 (Branding)

You run a small company that you would like to become better known. You have around 1000 connections and a company page with only a handful of followers that you are not posting much from because it doesn't seem to get the engagement you want.

- **Connecting** – Make a serious effort to increase your connection numbers as the current number is insufficient to gain real traction. Aim for 5000. Connect to all the appropriate decision-makers at the companies you're interested in attracting. When connecting, make sure you target the right audience and always send a personalised message. Follow up with a personalised thank you, via voice message if at all possible.

- **Posting** – Write and publish a range of information rich posts using all formats: text, video, image and document posts, and polls. Post some from your company page and some from your personal profile, differentiating between the two. How you do this will depend on your type of business but posts from your profile can be more personal and those from the company page can be more industry focused. Between your personal profile and company page, post 4–5 times a week. Build followers of your company page.

Invite your target market and potential clients to follow but give them a reason to follow by regularly posting quality content they will want to read. Steer away from being overtly promotional and always aim to add value. When posting from your company page make sure all your employees engage with the post to increase viewership. (There's a feature that alerts staff to the post, but at present it can be used only once a week so you'll need another messaging method, too.)

- **Engaging** – To maximise the reach given you by the algorithm, respond to comments left on your posts even with the minimum of a like. Have your staff members engage with company page posts to maximise reach. Share the post to your personal profile and seek engagement on it there, too. When you or other employees are posting from your own profiles, engage with those posts as the company page (see Appendix D for how to do this) so your logo is seen widely on LinkedIn where it matters.

- **Direct messaging** – Reuse content by sending connections high-quality content, perhaps in advance of it being uploaded to LinkedIn, so they feel privileged to read it first. Or, send material you have not used elsewhere. Where it makes sense to do so, invite response.

Scenario 4 (Building personal brand recognition, speaking)

You are in the coaching, speaking or training fields, working on your own behalf. It is your knowledge, experience and skill that people buy but you want to move up a level and be seen as a potential keynote speaker for large conferences and events.

- **Connecting** – Your network size and makeup will be critical. It needs to be large – with thousands of connections. If you specialise in a particular industry, real estate for instance, target people working in that industry, no matter what their role. Find a reason for them to connect with you and send personalised messages. If you have the resources, send the maximum of 75 invites per day. Withdraw any unanswered invites after four weeks as that person clearly does not want to connect or has not spotted your invitation, which means they are not active on the platform.

- **Posting** – Write and post thoughtful content. Articles are an excellent forum for this because they build into a library. Posts are less permanent unless added to the Featured section of your profile. Use posts to point people in the direction of your articles to gain greater reach. If you are aiming at public speaking, post videos of yourself presenting at events or share content from them. When event organisers are choosing potential speakers, videos help them decide if you are the calibre they are looking for and whether your message is something their audience needs to hear. Add videos to your personal profile, too.

- **Engaging** – Generally, well-known people generate plenty of engagement on their content; you will need to do the same. For this, you may need some help from your supporter network or tribe.

- **Direct messaging** – Depending on your level of confidence and faith in your ability, you may be happy to direct message those you feel could use your services at their next event. Plan this carefully, provide quality material so you appear professional, personalise your messages and don't spam. Some people are perfectly happy promoting themselves heavily without developing a relationship first and being sure the person wants to hear from them. If that's you, go for it. I'm more a believer in giving first to establish trust with a person before reaching out with how I could help them. Each to their own.

Scenario 5 (Cause)

You run a non-profit which isn't as well-known as you would like. It's an important cause but not a headline generator like the climate crisis or health. Your aim is to promote the cause, find supporters and develop relationships with capability partners who will be willing to help you, preferably pro bono.

- **Connecting** – Using LinkedIn's search function, look for people with large networks who, by their online activity, indicate they are cause-friendly. Connect with them in a genuine, low-key way. At the same time, identify the skills you need (e.g. website hosting or copywriting) and find people with those skills. Connect to them also in a low-key way, initiating a conversation that is about them, not about you. Nurture this relationship in an authentic way.

- **Posting** – Publish regular stories via posts about the work you do, the people you help and how it makes the world a better place. Look for deeper benefits than merely the obvious. Add lots of videos and photos related to your cause so people gain a better understanding. Ask for help only rarely in the same way it is not advisable for a company to constantly promote itself. Feature other people giving their time for the cause and thank them.

- **Engaging** – Create strong engagement around your posts and respond to every comment. Ask to connect to commenters who do not already follow you or are not connected with you. Operate from your personal profile, although you should also have a company page for your organisation, in order to get the greatest reach and highest visibility. Ask your best supporters to engage on your posts to assist this.

- **Direct messaging** – Nurture your relationship with connections to determine who might be a candidate for helping you in the particular ways you need. Not everyone will be able to give you money, some will instead offer their services free. Never take this relationship for granted or be rude if you feel they are not being as helpful as you would like. They will just block you and you will lose any goodwill you have previously generated. Also, LinkedIn is a public forum and you don't want them badmouthing you online.

Scenario 6 (Social media newcomer)

Your company has not dipped its toes into social media yet. In fact, you're not convinced it is even needed as you have primarily traded off referrals and word of mouth for the past decade or two. But you realise the world has changed and that to survive you will have to do things differently. Your service offering is increasingly relevant in the current market, and as you have heard good things about LinkedIn, you decide to dip your toe in the water. Where do you start?

- **Account set up** – Before starting any of the activities in this book, set up a LinkedIn profile in your own name and a page for your company. There is a checklist in Appendix B that will help you. If you already have an account but it has been inactive, reactivate it. Do not yet accept any outstanding connection invites or send any, despite the temptation to do so.

- **Connecting** – Once your profile is at All Star level, begin to connect with people. If you have outstanding connection invites, accept those that are relevant to your business or people you know personally. Be judicious and do not accept people just because they have invited you. You are in the fortunate position of being able to build a very strong network from scratch so make every connection count. As a baseline, do not connect with people who have no photo, fewer than 350 connections or whose profile is in the name of a company, not a person.

- **Engaging** – As you become more familiar with the platform begin engaging on content in the newsfeed. Provide helpful, constructive comments that make you look good.

- **Posting** – Do not be tempted to post until you have quality material available and can post consistently. If content marketing is new to you, engage a professional to ensure a flow of error-free and value-added posts and articles. Make a plan, set publication deadlines and commit to the process for at least six months. Measure the results.

A simple strategy for promoting a business to a target market

- Connect to all the appropriate decision-makers at the companies you're interested in doing business with.

- Increase your connection numbers with targeted prospects, working toward a base of at least 1000.

- Engage with people in your network. Comment on their posts and re-share their material.

- Start posting yourself. Develop a library of posts and articles that will attract people to your profile. But be careful to add value; don't promote.

- Build followers of your company page. Invite your target market and potential clients to follow but …

- Give them a reason to follow by regularly posting quality content they will want to read. Steer away from being overtly promotional and always aim to add value.

- When posting from your company page make sure all your employees engage with the post to increase viewership.

- When you or other employees are posting from your own profiles, engage with those posts as your company page so your logo is seen widely on LinkedIn where it matters. See instructions for commenting as your company page in Appendix D.

Summary

All the strategies detailed in this book – connecting, publishing, engaging and direct messaging – can be used separately or, as discussed in this chapter, combined for greater effect. Choosing one to begin and implementing it successfully and sustainably before adding others, is the key. For instance, you might publish the most interesting content in the world, but if you are connected to only a few other LinkedIn members, your audience will be small and the results unimpressive. Instead, it would make sense to increase connection numbers first to ensure greater viewership of your material.

The strategies you choose will depend on your type of organisation, objectives and resources. Some of the strategies take more time to put in place and to maintain, others can be used in a more ad hoc manner. Some you may be able to do yourself, others might require additional resources in order to be effective.

But what all these strategies have in common is this: they are not difficult or complicated to implement. They do not require advanced understanding of the technology behind the platform. All that is needed is an interest in reaching out to others, a desire to share information, and a commitment to try the strategies to determine which one best suits what you are attempting to do. If, after time, the results are not what you are looking for, move on and try another strategy until you find one (or two or …) that works for you.

Watch how others use the platform and if they are getting results, try their techniques yourself. Always be measuring and evaluating results so you can decide what works best, and then leverage the power of LinkedIn even more.

Checklist

Choosing the right strategy/ies for your needs

In the left column, list your objectives. In the right, place a tick under the tactic if it will be useful in helping you reach your objective. The first line is an example.

Objective	Strategy			
	Connecting	Engaging	Posting	Direct Messaging
To build a presence on LinkedIn	✓	✓	✓	

Appendix A
Reasons to be on LinkedIn
(Dr Joy Madden, reprinted with permission)

There are many reasons why people choose to be on LinkedIn. These are a few of them.

Promoting yourself and your activities:

- To house a succinct professional profile
- To establish a digital reputation (who you are and what you do)
- To develop and/or improve your web presence
- To build a personal reputation (expertise, authority)
- To show what you can offer (products, services, etc.)
- To publicise your awards, honours and certifications
- To get found for your specific knowledge and skills
- To become a LinkedIn thought-leader or influencer
- To share with others how you can help them achieve what they want
- To create content (articles, blogs, publications, etc.) that others might be interested in
- To highlight your personal assets (achievements, creditability, ethics, personality, etc.)

Connecting with others:

- To connect with new people to build relationships
- To connect with people before meeting them
- To get found by people looking for you
- To meet people with similar interests, e.g., via groups
- To meet people with different interests, again, via groups
- To get endorsed for specific skills
- To request testimonials that give you greater credibility
- To connect with influencers, thought-leaders and other 'experts'
- To connect with anyone you wish in the world with no real barriers
- To get introduced to people you may never have thought of contacting
- To connect with people who you could never meet in person (due to distance, disability, etc.)

Acquiring or accessing information:

- To find someone you know
- To find influencers to follow
- To find out what groups people belong to
- To search for people you have lost contact with
- To find people who can address your specific needs
- To find out who might be interested in what you can offer
- To access new tools, and training and development programmes
- To seek people for referrals, endorsements, recommendations, etc.
- To find out about someone before you contact them or meet in person

Businesses and companies:

- To advertise new products
- To create new partnerships
- To grow a business or company
- To find a new job or change careers
- To find further business opportunities
- To promote a business or company
- To increase a network of business contacts
- To acquire strategies for developing a business or company
- To find prospective candidates to join a business or company

Personal development and intellectual stimulation:

- To develop your creativity
- To help create your brand
- To liaise with kindred spirits
- To learn from other members
- To join groups that capture your interest
- To find mentors for your various activities
- To develop your personal growth in new areas
- To experience (and develop) new ways of thinking
- To act in an advisory or mentorship capacity to help others

Keeping in the know:

- To learn about new trends
- To find local events and activities
- To keep up to date with industry news
- To keep up to date with current affairs

- To keep up to date with general news (local, regional, global)
- To keep in touch with developments in your field
- To keep in touch with what your connections are doing
- To share information (knowledge, experiences, ideas, concerns and other issues)

Financial:

- To seek financial support for your activities
- To show others how to make some money
- To show others how they can save money
- To develop partnerships (joint venture, B2B, etc.)
- To generate new leads to ultimately make money
- To send traffic to your website with the view to selling something

Appendix B
Account set-up checklist

Set up your LinkedIn account in your own name, not your company's.

Display your legal name on your profile, not any other moniker you might go by unless you have an Anglicised version of your birth name that you are known by.

Add any academic letters you normally use such as MD after your surname.

Claim your personal LinkedIn URL so that it reads **www.linkedin.com/in/yourname** rather than **www.linkedin.com/in/yourname-23063587**.

Include your business email rather than your personal one in the Contact section.

Set up notifications so you receive emails detailing activity you want to know about. Hint: notifications of birthdays and job anniversaries might not be at the top of your list of priorities.

Set your privacy settings so your profile is open to anyone on or off LinkedIn who wants to view it.

Appendix C
Personal profiles –
an overview

To effectively implement the strategies in this book, you will first need a fully complete and attention-grabbing personal profile. If your profile is poor, any other activity will merely draw attention to that fact, reflecting badly on you. While people may be interested in what you write or post on LinkedIn, those who are interested in *you* will look at your profile. So, if your posts are interesting and intelligent but your profile is incomplete and doesn't tell your story or is riddled with mistakes, you will not stand out in a positive and professional light.

Another significant reason to have a high-quality profile is that whenever someone Googles your name, one of the top search results will be your LinkedIn profile – no matter how good or bad it is! LinkedIn is where every member of the business community goes to check out those they have met, are thinking of doing business with or just because they're interested in that person's background. With so many people now on LinkedIn, it is no longer good enough to have an incomplete or CV-style profile. If you want to know more about how to create a profile that stands out, download my free e-book at wordwizard.co.nz/book-resources.

Appendix D
How to comment/engage
from a company page

In chapter 3 I wrote about commenting from personal profiles. However, this isn't the only option. It is also possible to comment as a company, from the company page if you are an admin. (If it is your own business this is perfectly feasible and legitimate but if you are an employee, get permission first.)

Engaging with a post has particular merit if the post is directly relevant to the company doing the commenting. An example might be a digital marketing company commenting on a post by a business owner who is discussing the difficulties of keeping up with technology changes.

If the company page that is commenting has a strong following (most don't), it can help viewership significantly both for the writer of the post and the company which is commenting. I advise discretion when using this tactic, not least because it is rather a fiddle although once practiced a few times becomes easy.

Here's how to comment from a company page:

- Go to your company page and find and copy the unique identifier (the set of numbers in bold in the example)

in the URL bar that looks like this: www.linkedin.com/
company/**14404785**/admin/

- Go to the post you want to comment on and copy its URL
  using the … menu at the top right of the post.

- Paste the post URL into your browser.

- At the end of the URL add – ?actorCompanyId=xxx – (with
  xxx being the unique identifier of your company page, copied
  previously).

- The finished URL should look like this:

  www.linkedin.com/posts/lynnairejohnston_announcing-the-
  best-linkedin-pages-of-2019-activity-6604462282594455552-
  zSwG/?actorCompanyId=14404785

Go to the comments section of the post, and you'll see the company
logo to the left of the comment box rather than your photo. But just
for this post. You will become you again on the next post unless
the same process is followed. The relentlessly helpful copywriter
John Espirian has a very good video about it at https://tinyurl.com/
raus7d3

Glossary

The definitions offered here relate to their use on LinkedIn, as opposed to their more generally accepted meanings.

1st-degree connection – a LinkedIn member who is directly connected with another, having been invited to connect and accepted.

2nd-degree connection – a LinkedIn member who is connected to a connection but is not connected directly with the first member.

3rd-degree connection – a LinkedIn member who is connected to a 2nd-degree connection.

Activity – the section of a profile that houses, displays and provides access to published posts and articles. Engagement with others' posts and articles is also displayed here. It is also a catch-all phrase for publishing and engaging on the platform.

Algorithm – the closely guarded secret set of procedures that underpins the working of the LinkedIn platform.

All Star – the highest level of completeness of a LinkedIn profile.

Articles – long-form posts that can contain media, text formatting, links and other elements. Widely considered to add credibility to a person's profile.

B2B – businesses selling or marketing to other businesses.

Call to action – often used at the end of posts and articles to persuade the reader to take action of some kind such as to visit a website.

Click through rate – the measurement of viewers clicking on a link to another website or page.

Comments – LinkedIn members wanting to engage with what they see in the newsfeed write in the Comments section. Widely recognised as the most important metric of success of a post or article.

Company page – LinkedIn provides the opportunity for each organisation to have its own dedicated page that houses organisational information and is a platform for disseminating information or news about and on behalf of the organisation or industry.

Connection invite – a message sent by a LinkedIn member to another in the hopes they will accept and become a connection.

Content – material published on LinkedIn in the form of posts and articles. Also more generally, material published in blogs, on websites and in other places that is informative and aims to educate readers about an industry, product or company.

Content impression – the number of times content is displayed in the newsfeed (when referring to LinkedIn).

Content plan – a document detailing plans for the publishing of material or content. It can include dates, topics, post formats and other useful information.

Direct messages – LinkedIn allows connections to message each other directly through the platform and these are known as direct messages. The abbreviation for this is DM.

Document post – a post with a document attached. It could be a Word document, a slideshow presentation, an infographic, a portfolio of work or something similar.

Emoji – the tiny faces and images used in electronic messages, on web pages and on LinkedIn. They have a raft of uses in profiles and on the newsfeed.

Engagement – this occurs when a post receives likes, comments and shares. Any member may engage with any other member's posts, whether they are connected or not.

Experience – the section of a LinkedIn profile where a person's current and previous jobs are detailed.

External link – the URL of another website or page. If the link is live it will, when clicked, take you to that page.

Featured – a section of a LinkedIn profile introduced in early 2020 that displays videos, images, website links, articles, posts, slideshows and other media.

Follow – a LinkedIn member can follow another to see their published material in their newsfeed. It does not need the permission of the person being followed.

Format – relates to the types of posts published on LinkedIn. These are text, image, video and document posts, and articles.

Groups – a once popular way for LinkedIn members with interests in common to publish content specifically for those members through a semi-private newsfeed. Not nearly as popular as they were once because of the proliferation of spamming.

Hashtag – words preceded by the symbol #. They are used to group content together and can be followed. Any word can be used as a hashtag on LinkedIn and the most popular have millions of followers.

Image post – a post that contains an image. These are the least successful types of posts and receive the lowest view numbers.

Link post – a post that contains nothing but a link to an external site. There is no text except, sometimes, hashtags. These are not an official type of LinkedIn post and are often used by those who do not understand the platform.

Live video – a new and not yet widely available form of video that is published online as it is recorded.

Native video – a video uploaded to LinkedIn directly from a device as opposed to one that is housed on another platform like YouTube.

Network – a LinkedIn member's 1st-degree connections.

Newsfeed – posts and articles published on LinkedIn that appear on members' Home pages.

Page – a company page (not to be confused with a profile, which is personal to an individual).

Personalisation – referring to a LinkedIn member by name when sending them a message.

Pods – groups of LinkedIn members who agree to engage on each other's posts. Some develop into strong, cohesive and supportive units where the members share ideas and experiences. (Against LinkedIn's terms of service.)

Poll – a type of LinkedIn post in which a question is asked and up to four answer options are provided.

Posting plan – similar to a content plan but shows when posts are to be published.

Premium – a paid LinkedIn membership.

Profile – the lynchpin of all LinkedIn activity. Each member has a profile which is unique to them and can be used to showcase their talents, demonstrate their expertise and detail their experience.

Promotional post – a post whose only purpose is to advertise, sell, market or promote a company, service or product.

Publishing – making posts and articles available on the newsfeed. Also known as posting.

Reach – the total number of people who each see a piece of content.

Reactions – another word for engagement, it is the act of liking, commenting on and sharing others' posts.

Recommendations – the LinkedIn version of testimonials, recommendations are important proof of a person's professional ability and knowledge. Valuable because they are accompanied by the recommender's name and profile photo.

Sales Navigator – a paid LinkedIn account which helps members search, prospect and find leads. It has a wide range of functionality but comes with a commensurate price tag.

Social proof – the concept that people will follow what others do. Hence the proliferation of reviews, ratings and rankings, and on LinkedIn, the importance of recommendations.

Social traffic – the visitors going to a website, app or mobile site from social media platforms like LinkedIn.

Sphere of influence – the people in your personal and professional network with whom your opinion holds some weight.

Tag/@mention – when a LinkedIn member is tagged or @mentioned on LinkedIn, their name turns blue and becomes a live link to their profile.

Text post – a piece of content that contains text only and perhaps emojis or hashtags. There are no images, videos or documents attached. It is the most highly viewed of the four post types.

Trolling – posting upsetting or inflammatory material designed to cause trouble. Not often seen on LinkedIn compared with other platforms where trolls can remain anonymous.

URL – stands for uniform resource locator and is more generally understood to be the unique identifier of a web page.

Video message – LinkedIn allows video messages to be sent to connections from within the mobile app.

Video post – a post that contains a native video.

Voice messages – LinkedIn allows voice messages to be sent to connections from within the mobile app.

Acknowledgements

While one name alone usually graces the cover, books are like icebergs – with much more going into them than is visible on the surface. So, this may read like an endless Oscars speech but without the following people this book would still be a figment of my imagination.

Matthew Mewse – the love of my life and husband who kept me on track during this journey and had faith in both the project and my ability to finish it. That you are reading these words shows he was right. Again!

Norm Cunningham – who travelled round the world not once, but twice, to help me turn what began as a motley collection of LinkedIn posts into a coherent narrative that I hope will convince you to use LinkedIn to achieve your business goals. He did so with endless patience, making me laugh when I desperately needed it and being honest when my writing required work. I am eternally grateful for his good-humoured badgering, being a stickler for detail and a joy to work with. Every author should have a pernickety Scot as their copyeditor and proofreader!

My knowledge of LinkedIn has taken years to acquire and my main sources are the LinkedInformed podcast host, Mr LinkedIn, Mark Williams, the relentlessly helpful copywriter John Espirian, who constantly writes about the technical aspects of LinkedIn, and Andy Foote who is always ahead of the LinkedIn curve. There are many others.

My LinkedIn comrades-in-arms have unselfishly and consistently helped, supported, inspired, coached, informed and queried my LinkedIn ramblings for the past two years and I could not be more grateful to each and every one of them.

Many books are started, fewer are finished. That *Link·Ability* is in your hands is in no small measure thanks to Jaqui Lane, The Book Advisor (thebookadviser.com.au/) who has been with me every step of the way. Her programme makes it possible to bring a book idea to fruition without being buried in the detail along the way. Great fun to work with, Jaqui had me focused on the end goal – sharing the information in this book with the world.

Michael Hanrahan and his incredible team at MH Publishing (mhpublishing.com.au) have expertly taken care of all the myriad production, printing and publishing details. The result is a book I can be proud of.

Angela McAuliffe of Angela Jane Photography (angelajane.photo) crafted an image of me that is the epitome of 'scrubs up well'. She did such an amazing job I hardly recognise myself!

Videographer Wayne Alexander of FYI Media (fyimedia.nz) always creates videos that make me look and sound like I know what I'm talking about and I am more thankful than I can say for his constant helpfulness.

Designer Ryan Helliwell of One Zero Design Lab (onezero.co.nz) dreamed up the funky cover graphic and expertly handled the inside images, making his input invaluable.

My superhuman team member, Cher Forgeson, somehow manages to keep all the different strands of the business moving forward in an organised manner while handling all the tech aspects of our work. How she does it, I'll never know but I am eternally grateful that she does.

There is an entire raft of people who have helped me along the way. They include JoAnne Funch, Alex Piroux, Jillian Bullock, Karen Tisdell, Gal Yefet and, as mentioned, Mark Williams and John Espirian.

I am also grateful to my many clients who have entrusted me with their LinkedIn profiles and marketing. Each time I work with a client, I learn something new.

Many others have assisted with my LinkedIn education over the years. Suffice to say that if I have ever spoken with you about this subject, I am grateful for your input.

Finally, this seemingly endless list of thanks would not be complete without acknowledging my LinkedIn connections. As I make clear in these pages, a strong network of active and engaged LinkedIn members is central to success on the platform. To all of you – thank you!

Lynnaire Johnston
Word Wizard

About the author

In December 2019, the Social Media Marketing Institute of Australia released its annual list of Top 20 LinkedIn experts for Asia Pacific. At number 11, Lynnaire Johnston was the highest ranked New Zealander on that list.

Lynnaire has been sharing useful information about LinkedIn and also her specialty – copywriting – for several years. Her practical LinkedIn articles are also ranked by Google. She consistently contributes posts and articles on the platform; runs free webinars; has a fledgling YouTube channel; and runs the LinkedIn marketing and copywriting business, Word Wizard.

Trained as a journalist, Lynnaire has worked as a radio announcer and newsreader, magazine editor, and as a senior writer for a large local government organisation. She has written for the automotive, not for profit, beauty, electrical + automation, and travel industries among many others.

Her previous books include *A Horse Tale*, *A History of Ambury Park Centre for Riding Therapy Inc*; and with Matthew Mewse, the Telephone Man, *Super Size Your Sales* and *Cold Calling Rules!*

Connect with or follow Lynnaire on LinkedIn **(linkedin.com/in/lynnairejohnston)** or follow her Word Wizard LinkedIn page **(linkedin.com/company/word-wizard)**.

About Word Wizard

Word Wizard Online Resource Library

The Word Wizard website (wordwizard.co.nz) is more than a repository of information about Word Wizard services. It is also a library of resources about LinkedIn that continues to grow week by week. From posts to articles to blogs, the site makes freely available the text, videos, webinars and presentations the Word Wizard team creates to help guide LinkedIn members to success on the platform.

Word Wizard services

Lynnaire Johnston and her team provide a range of training and done-for-you services that help guide businesses and professionals to success online, and in particular LinkedIn.

LinkedIn services include corporate training, individual coaching, personal profile updates, company pages and a comprehensive marketing programme for those serious about using the platform to underpin their personal, business and career success.

Copywriting services centre around website copy and editorial-style articles (known as content) for social media, websites and media.

For enquiries around LinkedIn or copywriting services, email: **info@wordwizard.co.nz**.

Endorsements

Lynnaire is truly THE LinkedIn expert. Lynnaire's expertise and insight into LinkedIn is second to none. Since Lynnaire enhanced my LinkedIn profile the daily views on my profile have skyrocketed. Lynnaire is fantastic to work with, and her work far exceeded my expectations. I highly recommended Lynnaire the LinkedIn 'Word Wizard'.

Ben Lester, Workplace Victoria

Lynnaire was instrumental in not only writing and curating a powerful profile for me but she has insights and understanding of the LinkedIn platform that set her apart from all other people and companies that claim to be experts in this regard. She is diligent, thorough and totally professional. I would have absolutely no hesitation in recommending the 'Word Wizard'.

David Hoath, GM Asia Pacific, 2 Mee

Lynnaire is an excellent LinkedIn expert! She has always given me the latest and very useful news, tips and features of LinkedIn that have helped me tremendously. Moreover, she is a genuinely kind and fun person to work and interact with. I wholeheartedly recommend her!

Tien Le, Dusseldorf

Working with Lynnaire can be credited as the single biggest marketing element in the business that has had the most positive effect.

Every week our posts get incredible reach and engagement. Lynnaire and her team keep their eye on the ball seeking out the best connections for our business and who we should align with. Their approach to these connections and the conversation we have is well-scripted, considerate and with the view to long-term business relationships that are mutually beneficial. I highly recommend Lynnaire's services.

Lizzi Whaley, CEO, Spaceworks

Lynnaire is a LinkedIn guru! She is extremely knowledgeable about how to maximise the benefits of LinkedIn. She showed me features I didn't know existed and an understanding of how the algorithms work to enhance connections and visibility. Our session was fun and practical and we made changes immediately to improve my profile. I got far more out of our session than I anticipated and strongly recommend her work.

Megan Brice, Integrity Solutions Centre

What has impressed me most about Lynnaire is that while she has a prescribed programme for achieving results with LinkedIn, she is also very flexible and adaptable in the delivery. She is also friendly and makes herself consistently available to help in any way she can. I have found Lynnaire to be highly professional and knowledgeable, and in short, I would recommend her to anyone seeking assistance with using LinkedIn.

Sridhar Krishnamurti, Expand Consulting

Lynnaire and I have been colleagues for over a couple of years and now we're working together. Her knowledge of LinkedIn and practical tips and advice are helpful and measurable, and I've passed many on to other clients. Lynnaire is clear, concise and thoroughly professional.

Jaqui Lane, The Book Advisor

Lynnaire is a brilliant copywriter and I don't know what I would do now without her expert proofreading. Apart from her excellent writing skills, she is a beautiful person. Lynnaire is always happy to share ideas, knowledge and provide advice. I love working with her!

Sonia Sanchez Moreno, Sylaba Translations

I met Lynnaire when I was struggling to find the right words to express myself via LinkedIn. Her questions were spot on, and it was nice to deal with a professional writer who understood both what I was doing from a technology standpoint, and what I was hoping to achieve strategically. Her writing skills are outstanding and she goes the extra mile to produce incredible results, at any time. She has been very helpful with any advice and a great communicator with lots of fantastic tips. I can ABSOLUTELY recommend Lynnaire!

Adrijana Monevska, Key Media

I was lucky enough to meet Lynnaire through BNI and was able to use her skills to create a LinkedIn profile for me. Lynnaire was able to create a fantastic profile using my limited previous experiences which has resulted in me being able to grow my network and interact with my connections and generate business opportunities. I am sure without Lynnaire's expert guidance I would still be trying to connect with the right people. I look forward to continuing my LinkedIn journey using Lynnaire as the go-to person whenever I need help. As a company we have also used Lynnaire's expertise as a Word Wizard to create content for our website and newspaper advertisements and we continue to rely on her skills to enhance our business presence.

Clare Perry, Investamatch

Lynnaire has worked magic on my LinkedIn profile. Moving from twenty years full-time employment with a juggernaut tertiary institution to part-time and the development of my new career as a freelance speaker, I needed to up my profile in the corporate/ business world. Lynnaire has delivered on every promise and I'm full of admiration and gratitude. With great professionalism and always friendly and available, I can't recommend her highly enough.

Ian Chapman, University of Otago

Lynnaire has a great ability to communicate often complex or dry topics in an engaging and entertaining way. I have read a lot of her copy and had her help me with my own. Lynnaire combines her great command of language with a deep knowledge of social platforms e.g. LinkedIn, to create content that attracts attention and that gets consumed. And to cap it off, she is lovely to work with and generous with her advice and support. Just who you need in your corner!

Patrick Boucousis, The Sales Natural

Lynnaire has been a fantastic help getting my profile sorted out, so that it attracts the right type of connections as opposed to just traffic. Her down-to-earth approach and wordsmith skills were invaluable in making the difference to from "average" to "great". Highly recommended!

Sue Irons, Positive Real Estate

I used Lynnaire's LinkedIn marketing service for several months. My initial brief was for her to grow my number of connections (which she was fabulously successful at) and to manage my LinkedIn posts (which she was even more successful at). I also referred Lynnaire to two of my business coaching clients to assist them with website content and flier content and design. I'm pleased to say that she made me look good in the eyes of my clients. At all times Lynnaire was easy to deal with and she added huge value to my business.

I have absolutely no hesitation whatever recommending her to any-body wanting a LinkedIn consultant – she seems to know everything there is to know about LinkedIn.

Chris Baker, PeopleMaps

Mrs Lynnaire is Amazing! She had the patience, will and knowledge to point me to a right direction while also helping me improve my LinkedIn profile and find new employment opportunities! I would recommend Mrs Lynnaire to anyone that needs help with personal branding and/or job search.

Marko Tomljenovic, European "Ivy League" Graduate